A FOOL'S ERRAND

A FOOL'S ERRAND

WHY YOUR GOALS ARE FALLING SHORT *and* WHAT YOU CAN DO ABOUT IT

— ROY COOK —

LIONCREST
PUBLISHING

A FOOL'S ERRAND

Why Your Goals Are Falling Short and What You Can Do about It

ISBN   978-1-5445-1626-4 *Hardcover*

978-1-5445-1625-7 *Paperback*

978-1-5445-1624-0 *Ebook*

To my wife, Bernice, who taught me only those things worth knowing!

And to Hyrum Smith, the man who changed my life:
without his teaching, this book would be unwritten.

CONTENTS

CHAPTER 1

WHY CHASING GOALS IS A FOOL'S ERRAND

Nothing creates more stress than when our actions and behaviors aren't congruent with our values.[1]

—DARREN HARDY, AUTHOR, FORMER
PUBLISHER OF *SUCCESS* MAGAZINE

I couldn't sleep. I was having panic attacks several times per week. Often, I'd wake up in the middle of the night, unable to breathe, thinking I was dying. My wife (Bernice) and I lived in a high-rise in San Francisco, and many nights after having panic attacks, I'd run to the window to get fresh air. This scared the hell out of me and Bernice.

---

1   Hardy, Darren. *The Compound Effect.* Philadelphia: Vanguard Press, 2010.

After visiting different types of doctors to find out what was wrong with me and enduring an all-night sleep lab, I finally went to see a psychiatrist. After explaining my present job and an unethical request, he knew immediately what the problem was—integrity.

I was a partner in a New York–based marketing company. After eighteen years, they asked me to lie on a deposition so they could avoid a potential court trial. I knew my choice was to lie or change jobs.

I was hesitant to leave my current company because I was earning a lot of money. I had drivers take me everywhere, flew first class, stayed in the best hotels, and ate in the best restaurants in the largest US cities. Frankly, I was spoiled.

It was then that I discovered Hyrum Smith and Stephen R. Covey. I read their books. Their words spoke to me. They introduced me to the concept of core values. For the first time, I understood that everyone is different and has different values. I also knew that I had no idea what my core values are.

WHAT ARE CORE VALUES?

So, what are core values? I've never seen a better definition than the following, by Dawn Barclay, a personal trainer and coach. (This is the definition I will use throughout the rest of this book.)[2]

> Deeply rooted fundamental beliefs. Guides that dictate your behavior and actions. The foundations of what is driving your decisions. Ingrained principles that help you declare who you are and what you stand for.

When I first read this many years ago, it hit me right between the eyes. I discovered my eleven core values and decided it was time to apply them to everything I did. My ethical dilemma at work would be a good first test on how living a life founded on core values would impact my health, happiness, and fulfillment.

First, I created a spreadsheet. In the first column, I entered my eleven core values. At the top of the next two columns, I wrote down my current job and another possibility—starting my own company with a wonderful partner, Vince Cucci.

I wrote a number between one and ten in each box as to how well my current job or starting a new company would honor that particular core value, with ten being the highest score. Then I added up the eleven numbers in the two columns. The result made my choice easy.

---

2   Barclay, Dawn. "Core Values." *Living Moxie.* Accessed August 13, 2020, https://dawnbarclay.com/core-values/.

I would become an entrepreneur.

Specifically, I would start a company in an industry that I knew well, fulfilling what I saw as a big unmet need by the major US packaged-goods companies like Procter & Gamble, Unilever, Frito-Lay, Kraft, etc. These companies did not have a reliable and inexpensive way to deliver free samples of a new product to their target audience. Free samples are very effective for a new and superior brand.

As I reflected back on my thirty years of experience in business (1963–93), I noticed that all of it was in this rather narrow area of marketing. So I may have known as much about this as anybody. I clearly could see the need and noticed that no other company was filling that need. And I had a partner who was a terrific guy and very knowledgeable about this area as well.

LIVING BY MY CORE VALUE OF INTEGRITY CHANGED EVERYTHING

I had a core value of integrity, and it conflicted directly with what my New York bosses asked me to do. Leaving was not a difficult decision. The spreadsheet and my nighttime panic attacks made that clear.

So, my partner and I started our company in 1993. I began making every career and life decision based upon how well they honored one or more of my core values.

Did I make the right move?

The panic attacks disappeared over time, and our company sales exceeded eight figures within five years. Six years later, at sixty-two, I retired, having exceeded my lifetime financial goals.

Living from my core values brought fulfillment, and peace of mind, that I had never experienced before. Next to marrying Bernice and developing a spiritual life, it was the best decision of my life. (And God knows, as you'll read later, I still had room for improvement!)

There are so many things that I credit to following my core values, including developing a strong spiritual life; being deeply involved in philanthropic efforts; creating a large, free mentoring group at a local college and teaching classes there; spending much of my time reading and learning; traveling throughout Europe while studying history and art; improving my health via yoga, long walks, and diet; and writing this book.

Fulfillment is more important than achievement. Values take care of all issues about how to spend your time.

—UNKNOWN

AN UNEXPECTED BENEFIT OF LIVING BY YOUR CORE VALUES: FINANCIAL INDEPENDENCE

I'm now in my second phase of life: retirement. But I haven't stopped living. I can now focus on those things that are truly consistent with my core values.

This second phase of life has been even more rewarding than entrepreneurship. I don't have deadlines and large financial obligations. I have no clients. No one works for me. Entrepreneurship was wonderful and challenging, but it does not compare to total freedom: freedom in time and finances. Every decision that my wife (Bernice) and I make is now made without having to consider either time or money. I now *only* do things that I love. Like Steve Jobs recommends, I say "no" to everything else.[3] I also do not associate with toxic people. None.

I now have spent twenty-six years basing every decision upon my core values, and I can't express the fulfillment and peace of mind that come with only doing things that are close to my heart. Now, I want to share that freedom with others.

My question to you is: how could core values change *your* life?

---

3   Mejia, Zameena. "Steve Jobs: Here's what most people get wrong about focus." CNBC. October 2, 2018. Accessed August 13, 2020. https://www.cnbc.com/2018/10/02/steve-jobs-heres-what-most-people-get-wrong-about-focus.html.

YOU SHOULD ALWAYS FOCUS ON VALUES BEFORE GOALS

If the ladder is not leaning against the right wall, every step we take just gets us to the wrong place faster.[4]

—STEPHEN R. COVEY, THE 7 HABITS OF
HIGHLY EFFECTIVE PEOPLE

Focusing on core values has worked for others. In fact, how could it not work? If you make your decisions and actions consistent with your core values, those values that are closest to your heart, you cannot help but find fulfillment and joy.

Many people believe that simply having the right goals will bring them the fulfillment they desire. They ask, "Shouldn't my goals make me happy?" In fact, almost everything I read and listen to that deals with self-help refers to the importance of goals. "Experts" launch into the best ways to achieve those goals: how much sleep to get; the importance of a morning plan; what one should do immediately before going to bed at night; why people should form good habits, meditate, and journal; and how to avoid pitfalls that can keep people from achieving their goals.

Much of this advice is very helpful, but all of it puts the cart before the horse. All the approaches in the world to help one be efficient and effective in achieving goals don't help if the wrong goals are picked. Choosing the correct goals is critical.

---

4   Covey, Stephen R. *The 7 Habits of Highly Effective People.* New York: Free Press, 1989.

Not doing so is a potential disaster. And how do you choose the correct goals? By focusing first on your values.

Always start with values, then proceed to goals. Always.

So, if we must start with our core values, how do we find them?

HOW TO FIND YOUR CORE VALUES

In teaching this subject to hundreds of adults over the last decade at a local college, I found that everyone has ten to twenty internal core values. Where did they come from? Some believe that they are present from birth, found within your DNA, and/or they are influenced by your family, parents, teachers, spiritual leaders, and early experiences.

Regardless, core values were certainly deeply ingrained *prior* to adulthood. In my experience, it is unlikely that they change much, if at all, after that.

To give an idea of what core values look like for an individual, here are mine, in order of importance to me: spiritual, family, health, integrity, value-based life, community, freedom, accomplishment, learning and teaching, resoluteness, and renewal.

You may think that almost everybody has somewhat similar values, but, no, that isn't the case.

In fact, I have never found two people who share all the same values. They may use a few of the same words, but how they define those words makes all the difference. For example, your "integrity" value is likely different than my "integrity" value, even if we did, indeed, both share that value.

How extraordinary to know that we don't have to look outside ourselves to find our core values. The values are found and defined within.

THE REWARDS OF LIVING BY YOUR CORE VALUES

Hyrum Smith and his partner Stephen R. Covey made a promise in their books and lectures: if someone makes decisions based upon and lives according to their core values, that person will have a fulfilled life and peace of mind. I've found this to be true.

Consider if someone had creativity as a core value. She would not be fulfilled unless a part of her life was devoted to something creative, like painting, writing, gardening, etc. If she focused instead on something that she read about in a book or blog that did not relate to her core value of creativity (or another core value), she would likely be frustrated and unhappy.

Time spent reading about and acting upon things that are not consistent with one or more of your core values is wasted and, along with that, frustrating. This explains why so many people are not fulfilled in their work and lives, despite their intense goal-oriented mindset.

They are engaged in things that have little or no value for them. Once they discover their ten to twenty core values, this becomes clear. They are astonished at the wasted time and inefficiency in their lives. Unfortunately, many never take this step. (I didn't take it until thirty years after I started my career!)

The secret to achieving inner peace lies in understanding our inner core values—those things in our lives that are most important to us—and then seeing that they are reflected in the daily events of our lives.[5]

—HYRUM SMITH

WHAT YOU WILL LEARN IN THIS BOOK

You may have seen this or a similar productivity pyramid:

---

5   Smith, Hyrum W. *The 10 Natural Laws of Successful Time and Life Management: Proven Strategies for Increased Productivity and Inner Peace.* New York: Hachette Book Group, 1994.

The base is your purpose, followed by your core values. Higher up are your goals and tasks. Somewhere along the line we've short-circuited and jumped directly to goals. That's putting the cart before the horse.

To paraphrase Covey: some of us are so busy climbing the ladder of success that we are not certain that it is placed against the right wall.

Why should you spend your time and effort on goal-oriented techniques and productivity hacks, yet fail to understand your personal core values enough to see you may be on the wrong path altogether?

No matter how well someone's approach may have worked for them, that does not mean it will work for you. We are all different. We each value different things. Even when we supposedly value the same thing, it may have a far different meaning for someone else.

Discovering how someone else with different values reached their goals will be little help to you without recognizing your own core values, first.

The good news is that you can continue using whatever goal system you may already have adopted. However, for you to achieve fulfillment, other than by luck or chance, you must go back and discover your internal core values. Then, you can work on goals that honor those values.

Fortunately, this is a process that has already been laid out for us.

The problem with not knowing one's core values is that we do not know who we really are and where we should be going. Without values, how do you pick your goals? Many goals look worthwhile of your time and energy, but are they consistent with your inner values? Will those goals bring you fulfillment and peace of mind? You can only know if you have already discovered your internal core values, and then selected goals that align with those values.

Perhaps some people enjoy great success via a goals-based approach. Maybe they are fulfilled and have peace of mind. These are few and far between; most will not be so lucky.

When someone does not know their core values, only by chance or luck will they select the right goals. That is why so many people who have been "successful" have written that success wasn't what they thought it would be. They are neither happy nor fulfilled, because they failed to start with their values.

After you have discovered your core values, every day you can look at every decision and action that you are about to make and compare it to your core values. That also means that before you read something or study something else or do anything, it should be consistent with your core values. Every decision that you make should be consistent with your core values. If it isn't, take Steve Jobs's advice: say "no."[6]

Deciding what not to do is as important as deciding what to do.[7]

—STEVE JOBS

For purposes of this book, ignore daily chores. Also, we must recognize that those with children and home-care responsibilities will have much less free time for using core values to plan their future. It's not that they can't use these principles; they will just have less time to move as quickly as others.

---

6   Mejia, Zameena. "Steve Jobs: Here's what most people get wrong about focus." CNBC. October 2, 2018. Accessed August 13, 2020. https://www.cnbc.com/2018/10/02/steve-jobs-heres-what-most-people-get-wrong-about-focus.html.

7   Isaacson, Walter. "The Real Leadership Lessons of Steve Jobs." *Harvard Business Review*, April 2012. https://hbr.org/2012/04/the-real-leadership-lessons-of-steve-jobs.

Of the 400 identified values, you will find that only ten to twenty are your core values. That's no more than 5 percent. A heavy percentage of things that you may read, study, watch, and do may turn out to be items you can reject as inconsistent with your governing values.

Hopefully, you're starting to see why this could be fulfilling and give you peace of mind. You don't have to spend too much time puzzling over whether to do something or make a specific decision. If it isn't part of your core values, simply say "no." Why would you ever do something that is not consistent with values that are nearest your heart?

Now there is a possibility that you might be wrong in the process of discovering your core values. You may miss one or two. You will probably discover that omission over time, if you continue to move forward with your core values. It is also possible that you selected a core value that simply sounded good or was one that someone else (like your father) wanted you to have. There are some tests in this book that can be applied to prevent that. Over time you can do the necessary fine-tuning.

Choosing your core values may be the most enjoyable and rewarding exercise that you have ever done, with unquestionably the biggest payoff. Hyrum Smith and Covey were correct about that!

Do you know what you'll see when you get to the top of your ladder of success? Ah, that's the rub!

Throughout this book, you'll be taken step-by-step through the core-value discovery process that I used for twenty-six years and that changed my life.

WHO THIS BOOK IS FOR

In my opinion, there is one fateful decision most people make after finishing school. Their primary focus will be entertainment or continuing to learn. I fear that 80–90 percent want mostly to be entertained.

This book is only for people who want to improve themselves—for people who want to succeed and be fulfilled, at peace, and happy. This book is for those who are goal-oriented, buy and read books, and listen to blogs on self-improvement. They are most likely doubtful about the best path for them. They may be older or younger, but regardless of their age, they won't be so immature that they're not serious and just want to be entertained.

So, I am after the learners. I want the ones who read books and serious articles on or about self-improvement. I am not after the person who spends over two hours per day on social media.

HOW THIS BOOK IS ORGANIZED

Each person may learn in a different way: Perhaps some like tutorials. Some like stories. Others may enjoy learning how successful people have used core values to enhance their life. So, you can see from the chapter headings that I incorporated all these learning styles.

If you only want the tutorial on finding your core values, go directly to chapter 2. However, I suspect that many, like me, want more than a simple tutorial, which only deals with the "how." Many will also want to understand the "why."

Earlier in this book, I suggested that most folks are following a fool's errand by focusing on their goals, first. I discussed the importance of discovering your core values and the difference this made in my life. Each of the remaining chapters in this book are outlined below.

Chapter 2 helps you discover your own ten to twenty core values. They have been part of you since long before you were an adult. These rarely change as you age.

Chapter 3 quickly examines the current self-help literature and the status of society's focus on goal orientation. This chapter also goes into more depth on the importance of prioritizing core values above goals, and it discusses why we have forgotten that core values are the key to success.

(Essentially, the leaders who taught and wrote about the significance of core values have passed away.)

Chapter 4 gives you very specific examples of three people and their core values: Benjamin Franklin, Hyrum Smith, and me. These examples give you a clearer understanding of what core values are and how others have defined their own.

In chapter 5, I share my own story. I only learned about core values later in life, after I turned fifty-two. In my twenties and early thirties, I was a failure, irresponsible, and broke. I close this chapter by answering the question, which are more important, values or goals?

In chapter 6 we look at what my psychiatrist said to me. It changed everything. We also take a closer look at one of my eleven core values, integrity, which played a pivotal role in my life and forced key decisions on me. Lastly, I show you a breakthrough I had a few years ago that helped me discover a far more effective way to use core values in my daily life.

After chapter 6, you will have everything you need to change your life. In this chapter, I share how you can use goal systems and productivity hacks with core values. While you could stop reading after chapter 6, there are more chapters that address important refinements. There are many great productivity hacks and goal-oriented systems that can work wonders when yoked to your core values. Why not look at your favorites as I have done and see how they can work together to make a difference?

Chapter 7 shows how combining the power of core values with habits can make a huge difference in your life. This chapter also discusses why you should focus on small habits to get the best results. We also discuss how you can make good choices without using an undependable ally—willpower.

Chapter 8 discusses three tools that can be used with core values: the Wheel of Life, the Matrix, and the Pareto Principle. Two of them are powerful and one has a great reputation, but does it live up to that?

In chapter 9 you learn how to find your purpose, your underlying "why," which is the foundation of our productivity pyramid. (This "why" is also known as your "definite major purpose" in other literature.) Further, this chapter examines common advice, such as "Follow your passion!" Is this truly good advice? (Hint: I don't believe so.) Then, we examine why self-knowledge is required for a happy life; knowing who you are and how others see you is critical to your success.

Chapter 10 discusses why self-knowledge is a requirement for a fulfilled life and the importance of finding the goals that are right for you. Let's look at it another way: what is essential in your life?

Chapter 11 looks at the relationship between philosophy and core values. Aristotle weighs in. He wrote what some believe is the best book ever written on happiness around 340 BC. We also discuss why you should consider becoming a philosopher, or even a Stoic.

Chapter 12: I thought you may enjoy an entire chapter on quotes about goals and values from accomplished people, many of them leaders in their fields.

Chapter 13 is the last word. Once you know your core values, you can focus again on goals that are consistent with each of those values. Your core values can work with any goal or goal system, but by chapter 13, perhaps for the first time, you will know which goals are most likely to work for you, which goals will ensure your fulfillment, and which give you peace of mind. As Hyrum Smith has said, and which I have discovered to be true, choosing the right goals for you is likely to give you true freedom and financial independence.

WHY AM I QUALIFIED TO BE YOUR GUIDE?

Successful careers are not planned. They develop when people are prepared for opportunities because they know their strengths, their method of work, and their values.[8]

—PETER DRUCKER, *MANAGING ONESELF*

---

8   Drucker, Peter F. *Managing Oneself*. Boston: Harvard Business Press, 2005.

I am retired from work and financially independent after a long lifetime of experience. I was a failure and near bankruptcy for fifteen years. This is not theory to me. I have lived this.

I have tried many life and productivity hacks. Some are wonderful and very productive. Yet, I have found over the past twenty-six years that living a life consistent with core values is the key to fulfillment and peace of mind. It can also be the key, as long as other traits that I will discuss later are developed, to financial independence.

Would I have reached fulfillment, peace of mind, and financial independence without knowing my core values? I doubt it.

I finally took the time to discover my core values at a low point in my life. Then I became an entrepreneur. My company exceeded $10 million in sales in five years, and I retired in another six.

In the last twenty-six years since that low point, all life decisions and actions have been made in concert with my core values.

My core values have helped me develop a strong spiritual life. They have helped me become financially independent and focus on other areas that are consistent with these values.

The promise that Hyrum Smith put forth came true for me (fulfillment and peace).

Here is some good news: you won't have to spend the many months that I did to discover your core values. You won't have to pay money for an expensive seminar program. I will teach you this in this book.

I am not motivated by the profit that could come from such a venture. I am motivated to pass along this information, because it changed my life, and I know it could change yours.

It will not interfere with any practice or goal systems that you are currently using. It precedes those systems. Any goal system can work with your core values. Know that your core values will significantly cut down the amount of unnecessary reading, studying, learning, planning, and doing, eliminating much wasted time.

I did not always have this knowledge.

When younger, I was envious of others. I wondered how they succeeded, and I felt that I would never be in that group. I worked hard and was, I believed, smart and achieved some success. Then at fifty-two, because of a tremendous challenge and a big health scare, I reassessed my life.

I was convinced that Hyrum Smith and Covey were on to

something. I still had doubts, but that all evaporated as I started making all decisions based upon my core values and said "no" to everything else.

Now my life is filled exclusively with things that I love, things that are in concert with my eleven core values.

It's not often that the most successful step can come from such a simple principle.

For those who are open-minded, welcome aboard!

CHAPTER 2

＝＝

IT'S TIME TO DISCOVER YOUR UNIQUE 10–20 CORE VALUES

This chapter will help you find your key values. My twenty-six years of personal experience and ten years of teaching this concept will help you get the job done. This step was one of the most important ones that I took in my life. It changed everything!

Here is a list of 122 values (out of the 400 total), which should suffice for almost anyone. Feel free to add your own if you feel something is missing.

Abundance	Creativity	Honesty	Renewal
Acceptance	Curiosity	Honor	Resourcefulness
Accomplishment	Decisiveness	Hope	Responsibility
Achievement	Dependability	Humility	Self-control
Adaptability	Determination	Humor	Self-reliance
Adventure	Discipline	Imagination	Self-respect
Aggressiveness	Duty	Independence	Service
Altruism	Efficiency	Insightful	Sexuality
Ambition	Empathy	Integrity	Sharing
Appreciation	Empowerment	Intelligence	Silence
Assertiveness	Enthusiasm	Intimacy	Sincerity
Authenticity	Excellence	Intuition	Skillfulness
Balance	Experience	Joy	Solitude
Beauty	Expressiveness	Justice	Spirituality
Belonging	Fairness	Kindness	Spontaneity
Bravery	Faith	Knowledge	Stability
Caring	Family	Leadership	Status
Challenge	Fitness	Learning	Strength
Cheerfulness	Flexibility	Love	Success
Collaboration	Forgiveness	Loyalty	Support
Commitment	Fortitude	Nurturing	Teaching
Community	Freedom	Open-mindedness	Teamwork
Compassion	Friendship	Optimism	Tolerance
Competition	Fun	Passion	Tradition
Confidence	Generosity	Persistence	Trustworthy
Conformity	Gratitude	Personal growth	Truth
Connection	Growth	Philanthropy	Values and goals
Contentment	Happiness	Playfulness	Wisdom
Conviction	Harmony	Positive	Youthfulness
Cooperation	Health	Punctuality	
Courage	Helpfulness	Recognition	

Below is the procedure for discovering your personal core values. Remember, you don't select them; you discover them. They are part of you and have been from childhood.

1. Mark the values that resonate with you. Do not choose one because it sounds good, or because you know your parent would want you to, or because it's one you've always wanted. Your first list should have no more than twenty to forty.

2. Next, reduce your list even further. I have found some techniques that can help you do so. Use the "Your Little Helpers" section below to reduce your list even further to ten to twenty values. Not every Little Helper will work with every value. For example, the I-beam test only selects those very few core values that you would risk your life for. You might risk your life for your "family" core value but not for your "community philanthropy" core value. If you're occasionally stumped, look up a value in a dictionary. If that doesn't work, you can provide your own meaning. You may also add a core value that is not on this list.

3. Do not worry about making mistakes in inclusion or exclusion. Over time, you can make any additions or deletions that seem appropriate.

4. Find out what each value means to you. A core value of "family" may mean different things to different people. Write out a paragraph that personalizes what this core value means to you. For example, I wrote the following

for integrity: I am honest, accountable, and reliable. I conduct my affairs to reflect that: I am truthful; I can be depended upon; I am a man of my word; and I am worthy of trust. Note that they are always written in the present tense: "I am," "I conduct," etc. You could also include quotes from famous people or anything else that helps you define your core values.

5. Organize your values in order of importance to you. The first value should mean the most to you.

6. Keep reviewing this list to make certain you are satisfied with what you have written.

You may want to spend a little time meditating or thinking about your results after each step. Don't be in too much of a hurry. You may feel differently tomorrow or next month. I expect that you may see some flux as you're reflecting on what you've done. The Little Helpers will assist.

Once you've reviewed your list, you're ready to start using your core values on a daily basis. Before making any decision or taking any action, ensure that decision or action is consistent with one or more of your core values. If it isn't, say "no." Simply don't do it.

Remember Hyrum Smith's promise thirty years ago: if you live your life based upon your core values, you will find fulfillment and peace of mind. That's a big promise, but it was certainly true for me.

YOUR LITTLE HELPERS

Here are some very effective techniques to help you discover or uncover your core values.

These Little Helpers will assist you in discovering your internal ten to twenty core values. You may have many more values, but in this discussion, we're only talking about *core* values. They are the foundations of your life. They define who you are.

From my experience, there is no question that one or two values that you like won't make the cut. For instance, there is one value I continue to come back to and debate. Is it a core value or not? As of this moment, and after twenty-six years, it's still on the outside looking in. I do value it but just not enough to call it a core or governing value.

Which of the Little Helpers should you use? You decide. Different people will prefer different approaches. My favorites have been Your Funeral, Very Upset, I-beam, and Rocking Chair.

1. **Attend your own funeral.** Envision this: you are invisible. You walk into a funeral. You recognize everyone: friends, work associates, family, but who is in the casket? You walk closer—my God, it's you! What would you want the others to say about you in their eulogies? What would you like your obituary to reflect?

2. **Examine yourself when you're very upset.** That probably represents a core value being stepped on.

3. **Consider peak experiences.** When you are enjoying something so much that the time seems to fly by, that experience or moment may reflect an underlying core value.

4. **Imagine an I-beam.** Picture yourself in a high-rise office on one of the top floors. You see an I-beam from one of the windows stretching across to another high-rise. What would you walk across that I-beam for? What values are so important to you that you would risk your life for them? (This may apply to only a few of your strongest core values.)

5. **Sit in your future rocking chair.** Fast-forward to when you're older and picture yourself on the porch in a rocking chair, thinking about your past life. What are you most proud of? What do you wish you had done? What would you do if you knew you had only six months to live?

6. **Think beyond basic needs.** Ask yourself: "What do I really want after my basic needs are handled?"

7. **Look to your inspirations.** Who really inspires you, and why?

8. **Meditate/sit quietly.** When did time stand still? When were you in the flow? That probably means that a core value was being honored in those moments. What are you doing during the time that you feel the greatest sense of harmony and inner peace?

9. **Walk or swim.** Exercise helps you relax and allows your mind to be free and open. Think back: what were you doing when you were unaware of time passing and free of any "monkey mind" thoughts? What activity put you in that state?

10. **Use the dictionary.** Which of the values on your starter list really resonate with you? Look them up.

11. **Ask a few friends (or colleagues).** Hand them your list of values you are trying to pare down. "Please put a check next to those traits that you think best describe me." See which values receive the most checks.

12. **Consider what is most important to you.** What people, activities, or other things have the most importance for you? What seems most important with each of your life's roles? Are there things that you keep feeling inner promptings to pursue?

13. **Ponder the moments without pressure.** What do you enjoy doing when you're not under pressure?

14. **Lean into your special abilities.** What talents or special abilities do you have? What do you do really well?

15. **Reflect on what you enjoy sharing.** What do I enjoy sharing with others?

DEFINE EACH VALUE

Write a sentence or paragraph that explains how you define each core value. You can even define it differently than the dictionary does. What does each core value mean to you?

You'll want to review these over time and fine-tune them if necessary.

Here is what I wrote for my "value-based" core value:

- I have core values that guide my life and give it meaning.
- I set my goals and subsequent tasks based upon these core values.
- I recognize that following my core values is essential to living a fulfilled life. "The unexamined life is not worth living" (Socrates).[9] (Note that I used a quote that expressed my feelings.)

PRIORITIZE YOUR LIST

If you are satisfied with your list, reorder them in order of importance to you. It's good to know what your priorities are. There will be times when you have several events that are conflicting. Your prioritized list will help you make the best decision.

Here are my eleven core values, in order of significance: spiritual, family, health, integrity, value-based life, community, freedom, accomplishment, learning and teaching, resoluteness, and renewal.

---

9   Plato. *The Apology of Socrates.*

If there are three events in conflict this Saturday, this list helps me know which event is more important. Of course, this isn't always cut-and-dried, but I've found a prioritized list is helpful, especially if an event that is associated with a core value is one that is not fun or my first choice! It helps to keep me honest.

IN CONCLUSION

You now know your ten to twenty internal core values. You have written definitions for each one and have prioritized them in order of importance to you.

However, I've seen many get this far but never succeed in integrating them into their daily lives. Many lack the discipline to take this next essential step. The daily process of setting goals and analyzing both your goals and actions in terms of their harmony with your core values begins. If you are consistent in this daily process, soon it will become a habit, and you will start to see a difference in your life.

All of the remaining chapters in this book will help you with this process. They were written to motivate you to take the necessary steps to actually live a life flowing from your core values. If you do the necessary work, you are headed down the road to fulfillment and peace of mind.

═══

CHAPTER 3

WHY CORE VALUES HAVE BEEN FORGOTTEN

For the rest of this book, each chapter will discuss a few different, but important, aspects of how values work for us. Now, let's look at why the benefit of core values has been mostly forgotten.

About thirty years ago, the concept of putting together one's purpose, core values, goals, and tasks as part of the integrated whole was given emphasis. It was determined that personal values had to be determined first, prior to determining our goals.

Two men, who were business partners, gave lectures and

wrote books and articles about core values and their importance. Stephen Covey wrote *The 7 Habits of Highly Effective People*,[10] and Hyrum Smith wrote *What Matters Most: The Power of Living Your Values*.[11] Both took different approaches.

Covey's book was more comprehensive and sold over 25 million copies. Smith's book was focused on core values, which he called governing values. The process outlined in my book was more directly influenced by *What Matters Most*.

The reason for determining values first is that, for perhaps the first time, thought leaders like Covey and Smith felt that core values were inherent in each individual. We began to understand that values are part of us.

This emphasis on personal values has lessened dramatically in the last three decades. Now, few understand core or governing values and how to use them. Few blog or write anything about them anymore. But when you get to chapter 12 (filled with only quotations), you'll see how many successful people have been aware of values and their benefits.

Today, most self-help material focuses on what the best goal system is, on what to do before going to bed, when to get up,

10   Covey, Stephen R. *The 7 Habits of Highly Effective People.* New York: Free Press, 1989.

11   Smith, Hyrum W. *What Matters Most: The Power of Living Your Values.* New York: Simon & Schuster, 2000.

when to journal and meditate, and many other productivity hacks.

WHY SOCIETY NO LONGER FOCUSES ON CORE VALUES

Why did much of the teaching of core values that was published in books and seminars, especially those by the FranklinCovey company, disappear? One explanation is that the two principals of the FranklinCovey Company, Hyrum Smith and Stephen R. Covey, the major drivers of this knowledge, retired. Covey then died in 2012, followed by Hyrum Smith in 2019.

We now see very few books, podcasts, or blogs about core values. It is astonishing that this has happened. Why do I say that? Well, if I told you that you have an internal compass that, when followed, would likely give you fulfillment and inner peace, wouldn't you want to make use of it?

If this is your cup of tea, there is a simple way to discover your core values. It does not take several years. It can be done in days. This book is your guide.

I hope that you now have a clearer picture of why core values are so little known and discussed.

FOCUS ON CORE VALUES, FIRST

Here's the rub: core values precede goals. We create goals, but core values are inherent within us, closest to our heart. Those who focus on goals first are chasing "things." That's the whole purpose of a goal. Those who focus on their values are all about "being." Being trumps things. Once you know your core values, you can then set goals.

Core values are understood to be an inherent part of each individual. Most of us have ten to twenty core values. Hyrum Smith and Covey wrote and taught about this to thousands of people throughout the world. Hyrum Smith even made a promise: if one bases his life on his core values, making daily decisions in concert with those core values, he will live a fulfilled life with peace of mind.

Hyrum Smith and Covey felt that it was foolish to work on goals unchained from a person's values. Why would anyone do that? Why would anyone devote their time, money, and resources toward accomplishing goals that didn't line up with their values?

If you have ten to twenty inherent core values, that would make up less than 5 percent of the total number of values (400+). That means that you have said "no" to 95 percent of all values. Steve Jobs would be proud of you.

What might have you accomplished if you had limited your

actions only to the 5 percent of all values that are inherent within you? For one, unrecoverable time would not have been wasted on a high number of decisions, activities, podcasts, books, articles, and blogs that are inconsistent with your values.

I started acting on my core values in 1993, after studying core values. I discovered the eleven that are unique to me and started defining them, testing them, and making all life decisions based upon them.

I retired eleven years later.

I exceeded my lifetime financial goals, and that was just one result. In other areas of my life, equally positive changes occurred.

A GOALS-BASED LIFE DISCONNECTED FROM CORE VALUES IS INEFFICIENT AND INEFFECTIVE

Why waste time focusing on inappropriate goals? Your core values relate to the things that are closest to your heart and hence will give you the most satisfaction, the most fulfillment.

Some have written about powerful and effective goal systems, but do you really want to do the thing right or do the right thing? You want to do the right thing. With your limited time, shouldn't you focus only on the things that are closest to your heart and critical to your future?

Effectiveness without values is a tool without a purpose.

—UNKNOWN

Have you noticed that there are differences between you and other people in terms of integrity, honesty, spirituality, enthusiasm, determination, interest in giving back, focus on health, diet, exercise, etc.? These come from the differences in values within each of us. It would be hard to find anyone who has all the same core values you have.

Remember the productivity pyramid? In the past thirty years, we have moved away from identifying our internal core values. We have ignored our personal foundation, and we have moved to being primarily focused on our goals and various productivity hacks. That is very inefficient and unfocused. If you take the time to find your ten to twenty core values, you will have a head start on someone who has no idea about their values.

If you don't start by defining your core values first and instead focus on your goals first, you become a goals-based person. How does a goals-based person make her decisions on which goals to pursue? By intuition, by what feels good, by what she just read (written by those whose values she may not share). That can often lead to success or failure, simply by chance.

How could following someone who has written about seemingly very good goals or productivity hacks but does not share your core values guarantee success? Can you be certain that someone else's goals-based system will work with your values? It may work sometimes, but are you willing to bet your life on it?

Some of the time when you are honoring your core values, you may experience what I call "flow." You may not be aware of the passage of time or events around you. You will start to experience fulfillment and peace of mind.

Fulfillment and peace of mind are unusual experiences for most and unlikely to be experienced much by those who have no knowledge of their core values. Of course, anyone could luck out and live according to one or a few of their own core values. Even a clock that has stopped working is correct twice a day!

It also means to begin each day with those values firmly in mind. Then as the vicissitudes, as the challenges come, I can make my decisions based on those values. I can act with integrity. I don't have to react to the emotion, the circumstance. I can be truly proactive, value driven, because my values are clear.[12]

—STEPHEN R. COVEY

12 Covey, Stephen R. *The 7 Habits of Highly Effective People.* New York: Free Press, 1989.

CHAPTER 4

—

THREE PEOPLE AND THEIR CORE VALUES

To help you gain a better understanding of what core values are and what they mean, I've included examples of three people with their core values and definitions for each value. (Each of these sets of core values has different formats since they were created by three different people.)

BENJAMIN FRANKLIN, THIRTEEN CORE VALUES

Benjamin Franklin identified in his autobiography the following thirteen core values, which he called "virtues," that he believed were most important to him living a righteous life. (All emphases added.)[13]

---

13 Franklin, Benjamin. *The Autobiography of Benjamin Franklin, The Journal of John Woolman, Fruits of Solitude William Penn, With Introductions and Notes: Volume I*, edited by Charles W. Eliot. New York: P.F. Collier & Son Company, 1909.

Temperance: Eat not to dullness; drink not to elevation.

Silence: Speak not but what may benefit others or yourself; avoid trifling conversation.

Order: Let all your things have their places; let each part of your business have its time.

Resolution: Resolve to perform what you ought; perform without fail what you resolve.

Frugality: Make no expense but to do good to others or yourself; i.e., waste nothing.

Industry: Lose no time; be always employ'd in something useful; cut off all unnecessary actions.

Sincerity: Use no hurtful deceit; think innocently and justly, and, if you speak, speak accordingly.

Justice: Wrong none by doing injuries, or omitting the benefits that are your duty.

Moderation: Avoid extremes; forbear resenting injuries so much as you think they deserve.

Cleanliness: Tolerate no uncleanliness in body, cloaths, or habitation.

Tranquility: Be not disturbed at trifles, or at accidents common or unavoidable.

Chastity: Rarely use venery but for health or offspring, never to dullness, weakness, or the injury of your own or another's peace or reputation.

Humility: Imitate Jesus and Socrates.

Technically, these are goals or commandments. They are not in the present tense as core values should be. However, they're as close as we can get to his core values.

HYRUM SMITH, SIXTEEN CORE VALUES

Hyrum Smith was partner to Stephen R. Covey at Franklin-Covey and one of the earliest and greatest voices for following one's core values. (All emphases added.)[14]

I love God with all my heart, mind, and strength.

I love my neighbor as myself.

I obey all the commandments of God.

I strive to be an outstanding husband and father.

---

14   Smith, Hyrum W., and Richard I. Winwood. *The Three Gaps: Are You Making a Difference.* San Francisco: Berrett-Koehler, 2015.

I am humble.

I honor the memory of my father and mother.

I foster intellectual growth.

I am honest in all things.

I use excellent speech.

I maintain a strong and healthy body.

I value my time.

I am financially independent.

I have a period of solitude daily.

I change people's lives.

I listen well.

I have order in my life at all times.

As you can see, Smith is a deeply spiritual person. You may not have that value. This system will still work for you.

ROY COOK, ELEVEN CORE VALUES

1. **Spiritual:** I am a Christian and live by those principles. I strive to love others as I love myself. I give to others to help them. I support others to make their life better. I lift others up so that they can develop a stronger belief in themselves. I love others since we are all one.

2. **Family:** I have a loving, spiritual, respectful, and growing relationship with my family.

3. **Health:** I am strong, energetic, and alert. I am flexible and fit. I eat a balanced diet to have energy, skill, prevent cancer, and control weight. I have daily prayer for guidance and peace of mind. I exercise to "sharpen the saw": aerobics for energy, fitness, and alertness and to walk and move without fatigue; strength training for a strong back and fewer injuries; stretching for flexibility, fewer injuries, fewer aches/pains, and forestalling ageing issues; and yoga for strength, balance, and flexibility.

4. **Integrity:** I am honest, accountable, reliable. I conduct my affairs such that: I am truthful; I can be depended upon; I am a man of my word; and I am worthy of trust.

5. **Value-based life:** I have core values that guide my life and give it meaning. I set my goals and subsequent tasks based upon these core values. I recognize that following my core values is essential to living a fulfilled life. "The unexamined life is not worth living" (Socrates).[15]

6. **Community:** I give back to others who are in need. I do so with joy. When I ask God, "Why did you not do

---

15 Plato. *The Apology of Socrates.*

anything to stop human suffering?" he responds, "I did. I sent you!"

7. **Freedom:** I am financially independent. I have developed an income that will allow Bernice and I to live at an undiminished lifestyle until we die. I have sufficient savings to take care of most emergencies for my family. This income will allow all our normal activities, first-class travel around the world, cultural events in the premier seats, and US vacations.

8. **Accomplishment:** I successfully set and meet meaningful goals. I regularly set goals in key life areas. I ensure that these goals honor my life values. I set short-, medium-, and long-term goals. These goals are *smart*: specific, measurable, action-oriented, realistic, and timely. I fix dates in my timetable. I measure my effort versus the goal (productivity). I assess and set other goals. Finally, I ask myself, "Am I doing the right thing, or am I doing the thing right?"

9. **Learning and Teaching:**

    Learning: I am continually accumulating new knowledge by design. I read and listen to gather knowledge in areas consistent with my values—I act in that knowledge to convert it to wisdom. I select books carefully. I listen to others with a loving heart. I try to learn and relate better to others. I have role models, study them to learn how they succeeded and what steps they took so that I can learn from them, and act on that knowledge.

I learn so that I can teach others, empower others, motivate others, and inspire others to reach their goals and dreams. I learn to gain knowledge and wisdom so that I can set better values and goals, so that I will know how to accomplish those goals more productively.

Teaching: I am nurturing others, empowering them to accomplish their goals and dreams. I am using my knowledge, wisdom, and accomplishments to help others solve problems, meet challenges, set meaningful goals/dreams, and set out a method for accomplishment. I teach others in a way to motivate and inspire.

I nurture as a partner and as an associate. I recognize that the greatest accomplishments come through interdependent relationships.

10. **Resoluteness:** I will not be denied. I am consistent, persistent, and determined.
11. **Renewal:** I have made the enjoyment of nature, music, literature, and the arts a regular part of my life. I regularly walk and open my eyes to the beauty around me; these things are essential for my spirit and refresh my soul. I recognize that beauty and recreation are essential to a rich life. I am not a saint nor an ascetic: I also watch sporting events and old movies (like film noir) on TV.

I have included these three examples of people and have published their core values so that you can see and understand what core values are and how varied they can be. Note that even the tense is different.

I did mine without any reference to the others. Six of my eleven core values are not shared by either of the other people.

Do these lists describe me (or the other two people) honestly? Am I living all these values? No, of course not. These are my core *values*. They are not always my core *actions*.

I try to honor my values in all my plans and actions. They are ideals that help me focus on the best plans and actions for me, but I may fall short in honoring a value. What then? I refocus and try again.

Here are the thirty most common core values as voted by thousands of people who took courses and read books by FranklinCovey. They are in order of popularity, beginning with the most popular first. Even though this list was published in 1992, it can still be helpful:[16]

1. Spouse
2. Financial security
3. Personal health and fitness
4. Children and family

---

16 Smith, Hyrum W. *The 10 Natural Laws of Successful Time and Life Management: Proven Strategies for Increased Productivity and Inner Peace.* New York: Hachette Book Group, 1994.

5. Spirituality/religion
6. A sense of accomplishment
7. Integrity and honesty
8. Occupational satisfaction
9. Love for others/service
10. Education and learning
11. Self-respect
12. Taking responsibility
13. Exercising leadership
14. Inner harmony
15. Independence
16. Intelligence and wisdom
17. Understanding
18. Quality of life
19. Happiness/positive attitude
20. Pleasure
21. Self-control
22. Ambition
23. Being capable
24. Imagination and creativity
25. Forgiveness
26. Generosity
27. Equality
28. Friendship
29. Beauty
30. Courage

I hope these examples and this list from others help you

understand precisely what core values are and the meaning that some have given to them. My aim is to help you discover, develop, and act upon your own.

CHAPTER 5

I WAS A FAILURE UNTIL I TOOK A BIG RISK—TWICE

Until my thirties, I was a failure and had few—if any—goals. Certainly, none of my goals tied to my core values. In fact, I knew nothing about core values.

Although I made some changes in my later thirties and forties, only in my early fifties did I discover and begin using core values in every aspect of decisions and actions in my life. Prior to that, there was no indication that I would ever be a success or would lead a value-focused life. I had far too many weaknesses and a lack of discipline.

In other words, there is hope for any person, regardless of their past.

How and why did I change? What attracted me to core values? How did I uncover the crucial question of whether values or goals are more important? Lastly, how did core values help me? This chapter will answer these and other questions.

CINCINNATI

My twenties were filled with failures. I graduated from college in 1963 and went to work at Procter & Gamble, the Apple of its day in terms of its success and being coveted by college graduates. However, I had no focus and few, if any, big goals.

I did not drink in college but more than made up for it as I started working. I remember being on a business trip in south Florida. As I was driving my company car back to Miami from an evening of barhopping on Friday night, I had drank so much that I fell asleep on the freeway and didn't notice the freeway ended.

I plowed through and destroyed some rather large and substantial highway signs. The police came but for some reason did not arrest me. Later, I had to pay several hundred dollars for the destruction.

Another time in Indianapolis, I awoke in my hotel Saturday

after another night of ribaldry and decided to drive somewhere for breakfast. However, I couldn't find the company car in the underground hotel parking lot.

I decided to get a taxi and hoped I could remember all the bars where I could have parked the previous night. No luck.

As Sunday night approached, I thought about what I could possibly tell my company: "I lost the car!" (adding helpfully, "when I was out drinking on Friday night..."). That answer may not have made me look too good, but I knew I couldn't keep it a secret.

I went down to the hotel parking lot one more time. (I had already done this three or four times.) There it was, hidden in an obscure section of the lot in a tiny but deep parking slot, surrounded on three sides with walls. It was virtually invisible unless I was standing right in front of it. Luckily, I wouldn't need an explanation for how I lost a company vehicle.

I lived in Cincinnati at the time, which was the home of Procter & Gamble. On Friday nights, many singles would cross the river into Kentucky for the bars. One night when I was driving home drunk, I suddenly realized I had driven from the freeway on an off-ramp into a bus barn at 50 mph. That was not cool. It was dangerous and irresponsible.

When I think back on that period, I painfully recall an irresponsible, selfish, inconsiderate young man who lacked any kind of empathy for others. I actually borrowed money from some women whom I dated even though I earned considerably more than they did. I was lucky that I somehow kept my job at Procter & Gamble; losing that would have had a very bad effect on my life, career, and self-image.

The soul that has no established aim loses itself, for, as it is said—he who lives everywhere, lives nowhere.[17]

—MONTAIGNE

SAN FRANCISCO

After seven years with Procter & Gamble, I quit working there and moved to San Francisco in 1970. I had grown up on the West Coast in Portland and had gone to college in Oregon. Yet, my favorite city was San Francisco.

Within one year, I maxed out every credit card and was receiving collection calls every night. I was renting a flat on the top floor of a luxurious house in Pacific Heights (one of the prestige places to live in San Francisco). Since I was living far beyond my means and was missing rent much of the time, the owner threw me out.

I ended up in a residence home for $100 per month (covering

---

17 Montaigne, Michel de. *Essays of Michel de Montaigne*, edited by William Carew Hazlitt. Translated by Charles Cotton. Project Gutenberg, 2006. https://www.gutenberg.org/.

all room and board). You can imagine what this place must have looked like. The room was tiny, and I was supposed to be sharing my little space with another roommate. Fortunately, he never arrived.

My new San Francisco job evaporated with the recession after six months. For three months, I felt completely "left out," a noncontributing part of society.

I finally got another marketing job but had my car repossessed on the first day while with my new boss. I wonder what he thought of his new hire.

WHY DID I LIVE SUCH A LIFESTYLE?

I am not entirely convinced of why I lived the way I did, but perhaps it was because I had no goals and hadn't put much thought into it. My first three and a half years out of college with Procter & Gamble involved continual travel all over the US. I had no home, and I was excited to fully experience my travels. In those three and a half years, I visited 160 different cities but only stayed for four to six weeks in twenty-six of those.

Still, I loved that solo traveling, even though I was spending too much money and sometimes drinking too much on weekend nights. I continued this pattern while living in San Francisco for a few years. I guess one could say that I was "finding myself." Part of this was great fun and part of it was self-destructive.

Well, one can only live such a life for so long and maintain any self-respect. In my mid-thirties, I changed everything and worked my way out of near bankruptcy.

WHY AND HOW DID I CHANGE?

How was I able to make such a dramatic shift?

For one, and probably most significantly, I met my future wife, Bernice. She lived a responsible life and felt strongly about not going into debt. She would walk two miles to work just to save the bus money. Secondly, how long can one stand receiving collection calls at work and almost every night, getting nasty letters from credit cards companies, or not being able to pay rent and other bills? Lastly, I had established myself in the city where I wanted to build my future (in fact, we stayed in San Francisco for forty years, until well after I retired).

I also had one big advantage: I did not work in a job where the best I could look forward to was a small raise every year. I was in sales. Salespeople can make big jumps in income if they are with the right company in a growing industry.

I doubled my income in three years and quadrupled it in six

years. That quickly moved me out of near bankruptcy and allowed me to start an investment program. Also, Bernice was a banker and an investment manager. That helped.

There was, however, a setback. I invested most of what we had in gas fields and an apartment house in Seattle as part of a limited partnership. I lost most of the money—$250,000. That did not help.

TWO UNETHICAL EMPLOYERS HELPED ME DISCOVER CORE VALUES

In 1975 (five years later), when I was thirty-three, the company I worked for did something unethical. They refused to pay me for ongoing business that I had developed. So, I departed for a small, very successful, New York–based marketing company, but I continued living in San Francisco.

It was a good move.

However, in 1993, after eighteen years, this company asked me to do something very unethical. Specifically, they asked me to lie on a deposition that may have led to a court trial (the dilemma I mentioned in the beginning of chapter 1).

As I shared earlier, I couldn't sleep, and I was having panic attacks several times per week. That was when I discovered core values.

Core values are deeply held principles and beliefs that are closest to your heart. They are what matters most to you. They are not chosen. They are inherent within you. Your core values define what is unique about you.

If you act in a way that is counter to one of your core values, you will be unhappy or frustrated. As Hyrum Smith and Stephen Covey promised and I discovered, if you live your life based upon and make daily decisions in concert with your core values, you are likely to live a fulfilled life with inner peace.

Why is it important that you know what your core values are? What difference does it make? Knowing your core values gives you purpose and confidence rather than making decisions based upon circumstances and social pressures.

I soon found out that you're less likely to make bad decisions when you know and understand your core values. Your life becomes simpler as you know what to focus on and, equally important, what to say "no" to.

After discovering my core values (in 1993), every decision I made from then, along with every action I took, followed this question: "Does this decision and/or action align with one or more of my core values?"

Now, twenty-six years later, I've read a lot about core values.

Yet still, I have not found a current book that outlines what they are, how to find them, and how to use them daily. Most "success" books start by recommending goals and productivity hacks. The "success" pyramid has as its foundation your purpose; above that is core values; then comes goals. Tasks reside at the top. A goal-based life untethered to your core values, as we mentioned in chapter 1, is a flawed way to live one's life.

Before I discovered my personal core values, I was like others: setting goals, random goals. I never knew which books, blogs, and podcasts should guide me. There was far more written than I could ever read.

Now I only read, listen, or watch anything when it is in concert with my core values. That eliminates over 90 percent of media. What a relief! I can stay focused on true north, the direction of my core values.

As we've discussed, most goals focus on "things," while values focus on "being." Spending your life chasing goals that may not be appropriate for you is a waste of time and, perhaps, a colossal misjudgment. Do not make that mistake. Be a smart builder. Build your foundation before you build the house.

Also, remember you don't pick your core values. They are part of you. You discover them. Look within.

VALUES VS. GOALS—WHICH ARE MORE IMPORTANT?

Let's revisit this since it is so important. If we read most of the self-help and life-productivity hack blogs written today, we see they deal with goals. For most writers, core values either don't exist, or they don't know what they are, or (and this is true for many of them) they do not understand their importance.

That's very unfortunate since a focus on values should always precede a focus on goals. Some will pursue goals for years that are inconsistent with their core values. The result will likely be frustration even *if* they reach their goals.

I always like to hear what accomplished people think on such matters. That doesn't mean they are correct, but I normally learn something from their opinions and experiences. Here is a thought-provoking quote on this topic. (Note: to me, achievement-oriented means goal-focused, and presence-oriented means being- or value-focused.)

Align your direction with your innate nature. There are broadly two ways to live well. You can be achievement-oriented, or you can be presence-oriented. While we're all flexible and incorporate a mix of both, different people are programmed for different things. You should know your place on the spectrum before choosing your goals.[18]

—RAY DALIO

---

18 Rana, Zat. "The Principles of Creating a Good Life." Zatrana.com. November 26, 2017. https://www.zatrana.com/good-life/.

I feel there is little else I can add. Everywhere I look, I see blogs, podcasts, and books about goals. Or I find clever techniques and hacks that suggest the key factors to success are when you wake up; what you read; when you do your "deep work"; how you prepare for your day; how you prepare for sleep; whether or not you practice meditation, journaling, and/or tapping into the subconscious; etc.

I admit that most of those things are important and can be effective. In fact, I use many of those tools, some of which I've been using for a long time. Still, all these tools are on the periphery. They are secondary, not primary. They do not follow the premise Stephen R. Covey embodied when he said: "Put first things first!"[19] Doesn't that sound logical? If only we knew what "first things" are. Well, when you start with your core values, you know!

Simply put, values are the foundation. (Some, including me, would even put "life purpose" or my "why" below values on the productivity pyramid. We'll talk more about that later on in chapter 9.)

If you don't believe me, believe Benjamin Franklin, Stephen R. Covey, and the other successful people quoted in this book.

Here's the bottom line: a focus on values should always precede a focus on goals.

19 Covey, Stephen R. *The 7 Habits of Highly Effective People*. New York: Free Press, 1989.

If you focus first on goals and life hacks, you will have no idea if what you are accomplishing is consistent with those inherent core values that are closest to your heart. In other words, you will have no idea if any goal achievement will bring you fulfillment and peace. It's likely that you won't find either.

Of course, you may, luckily, find fulfillment or peace or both.

Whenever luck is involved, I always think of Clint Eastwood as Dirty Harry, aiming his large handgun at a wounded crook. While pondering aloud if he has any bullets still remaining in the chamber, he asks the bad guy, "You've got to ask yourself one question: 'Do I feel lucky?'"

Like the bad guy, I don't feel lucky enough to risk my life. I would rather depend on my core values, as I did twenty-six years ago. Because, when we set goals that are inconsistent with our inner or core values, we cannot guarantee fulfillment or happiness. Further—as I found—we may suffer frustration and even health issues.

Imagine putting years, and eventually decades, working toward goals that are not right for us. If you don't know the ten to twenty core or governing values that have been part of you since childhood, it is highly unlikely that you will be "lucky." After all, there are over 400 values, and you and I only have only ten to twenty. The chances are slim you will hit all, or most, of them throughout your life.

Now, what if you are in a bad situation currently (e.g., a bad job or marriage or relationship) that makes it difficult or impossible for every decision and action to be consistent with your newly discovered core values? Or what if you feel that some family members are toxic? Those are problems.

I can only suggest that you do the best you can in honoring your core values until you are in a better situation. Thankfully, a bad situation does not usually affect all your core values. Plus, it is critical that you move toward the light as quickly as possible.

Being able to quit things that don't work is integral to being a winner.[20]

—TIM FERRISS, *THE 4-HOUR WORKWEEK*

HOW CORE VALUES HAVE HELPED ME

What lies behind us and what lies before us are tiny matters compared to what lies within us.[21]

—HENRY STANLEY HASKINS

As I discovered through my own life, being a failure for many years is not a handicap. In fact, failing may be an advantage—

---

20 Ferriss, Tim. *The 4-Hour Work Week: Escape 9–5, Live Anywhere, and Join the New Rich.* New York: Crown Publishers, 2007.

21 Haskins, Henry Stanley. *Meditations in Wall Street.* New York: William Morrow & Company, 1940.

it tends to make us willing to change and adopt a new way of life. Also, something I found helpful in turning from failure to success was learning that the answer was within me. Plus, it didn't hurt to see that two of the most exciting thinkers and writers of their day, Stephen R. Covey and Hyrum Smith, both achieved enormous success by wielding the power of internal core values.

I only had to ask myself one question: "Will it work for me?"

CHAPTER 6

====

MY PSYCHIATRIST HANDED ME A BLANK SHEET OF PAPER AND SAID...

I used core values for the last eleven years of my working life (1993–2004). Then I retired, and my life became completely different.

In this chapter, we will explore how core values affect my decision-making in my new, retired life. Next, I look closely at one particular core value (integrity) that forced two critical career changes at low points in my life. Honoring this one core value has changed my life, making decisions easier and eliminating dilemmas.

I close out this chapter by showing you how to use your core values in the day-to-day: I show you how to use your file manager and task manager (or to-do list) to decide which daily decisions and actions should be taken. (This eliminates the need for the discipline that it would normally take to keep you and I focused on our core values. Making this simple tweak to the way you use your file and task managers is a game-changer!)

First, much of what is written about retirement is incorrect; I retired from entrepreneurship in 2004. When that happened, I took advice from a wise man. He handed me a blank sheet of paper and said, "You can design a new life. For the first time, you can do exactly what you want to do and only what you want to do."

He told me to spend time considering my values, then choose activities that honored those values. "Take your time, and don't get back on the horse for a while!" he said.

Fortunately, I already knew what my eleven core values were. I had spent many months determining what they were eleven years earlier during the period of crisis in my life.

I took the advice of this wise man. I read and studied for about a year. At the end of that time, I had a handful of activities that fit the bill in three ways:

1. They honored my core values.
2. I really wanted to do them.
3. They had nothing to do with my prior career.

What came next was (and still is) glorious fulfillment. I spend time each day doing only those things that I love. I make choices in line with my core values—even down to the amount of time I spend on each activity.

Some say that when you retire from your career, you will vegetate, become bored, lose interest in life, die early. That depends on who you are and what you retire *to*. If you don't know what is ahead after you retire, then, yes, you may be in trouble, but how did it work out for me?

Before I retired, the best part of my career life had been the last eleven years, as an entrepreneur. Yet, since retirement, I spend time doing only what I want to do, activities that honor my core values.

No matter what your career is, at least some of your time is not fun. For me, that is no longer true.

The most significant difference for me between career and post-career activities is that the latter generally does not involve stress, money, dealing with people I don't like, or doing some things that I don't like.

Yes, I loved my entrepreneurial career but not all of it. In my current situation, I ruthlessly follow Steve Jobs' dictum "learn how to say 'no.'" It's a wonderful freedom to have.

I also now head three groups:

1. A group of fraternity brothers that meets biannually to focus on children's education: My fraternity brothers and I had lost contact with each other for forty years, before I helped bring us back together in 2003. Now, eighteen fraternity brothers and our spouses meet together to discuss and act on children's education and other, more personal matters. Until 2003, when we all began to reconnect, none of us had any sustained relationships with each other since college. Now, what we have are fulfilling, life-giving relationships that benefit us and the community around us. The alumni director at our university said he knew of no other fraternal group where almost all members were meeting regularly after being away from college for several decades.

2. A large mentoring program at a local college: three of us match adults with vast career and life experience from Osher Lifelong Learning Institute (OLLI) with college students who need and want mentoring. (OLLI is a nationwide educational program at major universities for those over fifty.)

3. Annual meeting with long-ago colleagues who have had minimal contact since 1969: I spend three days a year

with two guys I met at Procter & Gamble, where we were starting our careers in our early twenties. We discuss things that matter in our lives: success, health, families, spirituality, life philosophy, and, of course, sports.

Does it sound like my life is over because I don't have a job or a career?

If you want fulfillment in your post-career life, you must open your mind and define "retired" differently.

I started thinking about this recently when I read a blog on Stoicism. Here's what I learned: I can't control everything that happens to me, but I can control what I think, feel, and say about it. (However, with my post-career life focused on my core values, I can control an increasing amount of what happens to me, too!) The result of this understanding is fulfillment and peace of mind, exactly what Hyrum Smith and Stephen R. Covey promised.

HOW I HONOR MY CORE VALUES

I thought it may be helpful for you to see how living by my core values in my retired life works (for me). Perhaps looking at my life will help you to look ahead to see what is in store when you live according to your core values.

Here are each of my core values ranked in order of importance to me (in bold), accompanied by my current activity(ies) that honor it:

1. **Spiritual:** I practice daily prayer and meditation. (The result of daily prayer and meditation is a more relaxed life, full of peace. I also have a better attitude toward others.)
2. **Family:** I am very supportive of my wife, pray for her daily, tell her I love her daily, and I have provided her financial security (if I die first, she can live any way she wants without any financial concerns). Also, we don't have children, or their emotional and financial well-being would be included here as well.
3. **Health:** I have developed a comprehensive personal health program for myself, which includes nutrition, yoga, and exercise. I learn from professional teachers in each of these endeavors.
4. **Integrity:** I have had two career changes because I preferred to quit my job rather than act unethically (1975 and 1993).
5. **Value-based life:** I organize my task manager and file-saver by my eleven core values. (Do not miss my discussion on how to do this later in this chapter; for me, this was a game-changer!)
6. **Community:** I am involved in philanthropic activities, including educating poorer kids in Mexico, in south-central Los Angeles, and on the Oregon coast. Plus, I have helped two families affected by Hurricane Katrina relocate to the West Coast. Also, I helped organized a

large mentoring program with adults and kids at a local college. I helped bring back together, and now meet biannually with, eighteen fraternity brothers and their spouses to do philanthropic work. Two men (who started their careers with me at Procter & Gamble) and I meet for annual meetings. Lastly, I wrote a book on how individuals can discover their personal core values and then use them to change their lives.

7. **Freedom:** This is how I live my life. I never thought that I would be "free." That means making all decisions without regard to cost or time. Specifically, two aspects have helped enable this freedom:

   A. Entrepreneurship: This allowed me to exceed my lifetime financial goals.

   B. Finding a top investment advisor: This has made a huge difference and provided peace of mind for both my wife (Bernice) and me but especially Bernice. Even though she was an institutional stockbroker, we never made our own investments. Now I know this: why risk peace of mind for a fee of less than 1 percent?

8. **Accomplishment:** Consistently living according to my core values has enabled me to accomplish eleven lifelong goals, many of which took decades to complete. I have listed them below so you can observe both the dedication required and the potential peace that comes from seeing a goal fulfilled that stems from one's core values.

Three of these took over forty years (which means that I

started on them before knowing my core values; however, I did have a yearning inside and, thankfully, sometimes followed that internal feeling). The other eight goals took two to eleven years, and, while I say that I've "completed" all of them, obviously, some of them are ongoing.

All of these involved intense dedication that included years of focused work and growth, much study, and sometimes travel. How many of these goals would have been accomplished if I did not live a life focused on core values? It's impossible to give a precise answer, but without focusing on core values, I know that my life would have been quite different.

The first word(s) is the core value that is honored by the accomplishment.

A. *Spiritual:* Developed a spiritual life and a habit of daily meditating and praying (twenty-seven years)
B. *Family:* Built a wonderful marriage (forty-five years)
C. *Learning, Renewal:* Gained some of the knowledge of a polymath—art, history, literature, religion, philosophy, music, dance (forty-five years)
D. *Integrity, Freedom:* Became a successful entrepreneur by filling an unmet national need of the top fifty blue-chip companies (eleven years)
E. *Freedom:* Gained financial independence (eleven years)

F. *Learning, Renewal:* Read and taught all the one hundred Great Books from Fadiman and Major's list in *The New Lifetime Reading Plan* (eight years)

G. *Learning, Renewal:* Developed a general understanding of Western civilization by regular and continual travel throughout the Middle East and Europe, Berkeley and Stanford classes, and continual reading (forty-three years)

H. *Learning, Renewal:* Taught a course on why the West became dominant (two years)

I. *Health, Family:* Created (and utilized) a healthy lifetime diet (four years) and maintained a healthy weight

J. *Community, Renewal:* Wrote a book on core values (two years)

K. *Renewal:* Overcame the shyness of meeting and dating women (five years)

9. **Learning and teaching:** I teach adult courses at a local college: Great Books, historical novels and bios, art, iPad, and *How to Find Your Personal Core Values.* I have also read all one hundred of Fadiman and Major's Great Books in eight years while I was teaching the Great Books course. I read and study daily: Great Books, historical novels and biographies, philosophy, and self-help books about success.

10. **Resoluteness:** I try to reflect this in everything I do. Besides accomplishment and the individually associated

core values, all eleven of my goals listed under accomplishments also honored my core value of *resoluteness*.

11. **Renewal:** Bernice and I take two European trips per year. Plus, we enjoy many plays, musical performances, lectures, top restaurants, etc. I read and study frequently, and I watch sporting events and film noir movies often.

To be clear, none of this happened by accident. All of these activities were selected because they were consistent with one or more of my core values. I considered and rejected many other activities that were not consistent. It made life choices easier.

You can see the clear definition of each of my eleven core values in chapter 4, making activity selection fairly straightforward. If you look at the list of eleven lifelong goal accomplishments just above under "Accomplishment," you can see the same pattern unfolding. Because of the extended period of time required to achieve lifetime goals, the fact that each of them is consistent with my core values allowed me to maintain the motivation necessary.

But how did I pick such activities in the first place? I made lists of possibilities. Then I compared each activity with my core values. Remember, my psychiatrist insisted that I do this when I retired in 2004. He flat out told me that I would not be happy if all I was doing was taking it easy: golfing, gardening, reading, walking, traveling, and other activities commonly associated with retired people.

He told me that I needed to be doing things that were of value to me. He and an associate told me to make a list of activities that were important to me, that might give me a feeling of joy. They gave me a few books to read on the subject. This was important since when I retired I all of a sudden had mostly free time. This was, in effect, a new life, a new life that could likely last up to thirty years.

How lucky I was to run into Dr. William Prey and his associate Dr. Kathleen Levdar in San Francisco when I needed them. They were invaluable. As soon as they both told me to only select activities that were of value to me, I knew what to do. I had been doing this since 1993 with my core values.

So, late in life, as I was retiring, my psychiatrist handed me a sheet of paper that changed everything. He prepared me for what I could expect. I used my core values to start a new life, one that had me only doing things that I loved, things closest to my heart. What a wonderful fifteen-year period.

WHY YOU CAN'T ADOPT ANOTHER'S CORE VALUES

By the way, remember that these are *inherent* core values. They are part of you.

I saw a book recently that dealt with picking your core values. That is incorrect. One cannot choose his core values.

Let us think about this for a moment. Could someone who is dishonest pick integrity as a core value? He might improve himself if he did so, but integrity is not one of his core values.

If you find goals, actions, or decisions that don't fit within any your core values, that's an indication they should be discarded or you've done your core values incorrectly or you may need to add a core value to your list or change the definition of a current core value. It could take some thought.

Remember: the answer is within. That's the beauty of this process, and that's why it works. These values are part of you and have been for a long time. They don't change much, if at all.

This is not to say that someone couldn't change herself and become more honest and reliable. However, if honesty or integrity is her core value, she would not have to make a herculean effort to change. It's already part of her. She just has to honor it.

Look within. Do not adopt others' values. The answer lies inside.

However, we can and should adopt others' excellent productivity hacks for accomplishing goals, if they are right for us. We all want to accomplish goals that are in line with our core values as quickly and efficiently as possible, but do not copy someone else's core values. They are not right for you.

A CLOSER LOOK AT CORE VALUES

Let's take a closer look at one of my core values and see how it relates to me. The top four, rated by importance to me, are spiritual, family, health, and integrity. Integrity would be on my list regardless of my life circumstances. Yet, why does integrity come in fourth place, ahead of seven of my other values?

Because I've seen its impact on my life. Remember my 1993 episode in chapter 1? (My business partners asked me to do something unethical. I couldn't sleep, and I was having panic attacks.)

Ultimately, that dilemma led to my departure from my business partners and became the starting point for entrepreneurship, which I loved. Owning my own business allowed me to act consistently with my core values, and, for much of the time, I did what I enjoyed as an entrepreneur.

Now, as a retiree, I *only* do those things that are consistent with my core values. Everything I do is enjoyable and fulfilling. Everything. For the first time in my life, I say "no" to anything that is not consistent with any one of my eleven core values. I still say "no" a lot.

Earlier, you read what integrity means to me: I am honest, accountable, and reliable. I conduct my affairs such that I am truthful; I can be depended upon; I am a man of my word; and I am worthy of trust.

This is not a dictionary meaning. It is simply what integrity means to me. Since it is a core value, I know that it is inherent and close to my heart. I have known this and operated daily with this knowledge for twenty-six years.

HOW DOES INTEGRITY IMPACT MY DAILY ACTIONS?

Here is one daily effect: I don't lie. Still, on a grander scale, there have been two instances where the impact of this value was more dramatic (i.e., the two situations at previous employers and unethical requests).

You've already heard about one episode. The other episode occurred earlier, in 1975, long before I had discovered my core values. I was living in San Francisco and working as a salesman for a national marketing company. I landed a large new account in Oregon. Normal sales up until then involved one project that would be completed within a one-month period. Salesmen were paid a one-time commission on that "job."

However, I sold this client ongoing large projects that would continue year after year. My company would owe me large commission checks every year without any further sales efforts on my part. Instead, my company president decided he would make this client a "company account" and only pay me for the first year.

That was unethical. I quit on the spot.

At that point, I knew nothing of core values, but nonetheless, integrity was one of my (undiscovered) core values. It was internal and had been present most of my life. I acted upon it, resulting in temporary insecurity but eventually a much better job and a partnership.

Fast-forward to 1993, and my superiors at the firm where I was a partner asked me to do something that was very unethical. I have already discussed it earlier. This time, I knew that I had a core value of integrity.

Now, let's review. Two times companies that I worked for tried to do something unethical involving me. What were the results because I had a core value of integrity?

The first time, I found a job I enjoyed and that paid better and included other benefits. Had I stayed with the unethical company, I would have hated myself, and my employer would have known that they could do anything to me without consequence.

The second time, I was faced with an unethical request, I became an entrepreneur and retired eleven years later, having exceeded my lifetime financial goals. That was a superior situation to my previous employment. As an entrepreneur, I ran a national company with a partner who respected my integrity. (We built a large business with the top fifty blue-chip packaged-goods companies.)

In both situations, I had to act on the core value of integrity, and it wasn't easy. The outcomes were unknown, and they could have created financial upheaval for my wife and me. I learned that it takes courage to act in the face of an unknown future.

Yes, knowing your core values is not enough to guarantee success. Other things are necessary. One must pick his career wisely. One must develop other success traits, like discipline and good people skills. Still, core values offer a strong starting point.

In summary, I enjoyed owning my own company more than being an employee, but nothing compares to being retired (from work) and only doing things that are consistent with my core values. Now, as a final reward, I am passing along what I've learned via this book.

THE FILE MANAGER/TASK MANAGER SYSTEM

Goals are good for setting a direction, but systems are best for making progress.[22]

   —JAMES CLEAR, JAMESCLEAR.COM, *ATOMIC HABITS*

---

22 Clear, James. *Atomic Habits.* New York: Avery, 2018.

Core values are like a sharp scythe. They cut down and eliminate task and goal clutter.

I had a breakthrough about five years ago. I noticed that some people in the classes I taught to adults for free at a local university were quitting the program after identifying and defining their core values. They lacked the discipline to apply their core values to their daily goals and tasks. As a result, their lives remained largely unchanged.

Core values are completed when you have a set system. Systems ultimately become habits. You need daily tools to ensure that you are following your core values with your decisions and goals. We need a *file manager* to keep valuable information and documents. We also need a *task manager* (or task list) to ensure that we are accomplishing the right activities.

I have used two apps for years: Evernote (file manager) and Things (task manager). They are now habits. I have also created a system that effectively employs both of these. You may use different tools. For example, you may store your files on your computer and simply have a written to-do list for tasks.

Below, I'm going to describe how I use the task manager Things and the file manager Evernote within my unique system. However, this system can be used with whatever tools you have.

First, let's recognize that everything that you do and will ever do involves either a file and/or a task. No matter who you are or what you do, all the elements of your work and play will be files and/or tasks. So that is why I'm going to focus only on file and task managers.

The first thing that I have done is to make certain that Things only has *tasks* and Evernote only has *files/documents* that are consistent with my core values:

- I use the word "tasks" to mean to-dos that are part of a project, whether it's for work, home, trips, etc. (So, items like "Send colleague an updated financial spreadsheet" or "Purchase paint for garage" would both be "tasks.")
- Files (or documents) in Evernote include Word/Excel documents. This is for items like flight/lodging emails, maps, articles, blogs, important email messages, lists, photos, web pages, trip plans, sketches, audio files, ideas, plans, etc.

Living by your core values comes down to a system, not just a hope. Not only that, but once you have a system, you can create daily habits. Those habits will ultimately propel you to a point where you can look back and see that your core values were lived out.

This system above was helpful for me, but I added a refinement that took this system to a new level. Most task managers and file managers allow you to create folders in which to store similar items. For example, all files that involve a business project can go in the same folder.

Remember that I have eleven core values. So, I created eleven folders in my task manager and eleven folders in my file manager. I named each folder after a core value. I then transferred all of my files and to-dos (tasks) into appropriate folders. I deleted all remaining files.

Every task had to fit in one of the eleven folders in Things. Also, every file/document had to fit in one of the eleven folders in Evernote.

If a task or file did not fit in a folder, I had obvious choices: either it was not worthy of my time or, perhaps, I had another core value that I had not considered. In the end, I had no tasks or files that did not apply to one of my core values.

Now, every day that I come across a document that I want to save or when I think of a new project or task, it must fit into one of the eleven folders in my task manager, Things, or it must fit into one of the eleven folders on my file manager, Evernote. If a document for a new project does not fit into any of these folders, I discard it. These choices cause me to continually reevaluate my core values, ensuring that the eleven core values are correct.

This has become a tremendous time-saver, and it has allowed

me to ignore tasks and files that are not consistent with my core values.

This small change has made all the difference for me: it has created a powerful system that forces me to only focus on tasks and files that are congruent with one or more of my core values.

SUMMARY

In this chapter, we reviewed my discussion with my psychiatrist and the life-changing result. We took an in-depth look at all my core values and their corresponding activities and achievements. We looked closely at one of my values, integrity, and how acting consistently with it changed my life. Lastly, we looked at a discovery that I made with my task and file managers that made it easier to live a fulfilling core-value-based life.

CHAPTER 7

THE POWER OF COMBINING HABITS AND CORE VALUES

You can use a variety of approaches with core values to achieve better results in your work and private life. In this chapter we look at two of them: habits and another approach that substitutes for willpower, which is a very difficult and undependable ally.

PART I: HABITS

I was so intrigued when I read two new books on the power of habits (see below). Habits, supposedly, would allow me to accomplish my goals without daily struggle.

So, I decided to put together a morning group of *stacked habits,* which is a series of habits linked one after the other without break. Stacked habits are a great way to get the day started by accomplishing goals "automatically." For readability, I labeled these habits by the room in which they occur:

1. **Bedroom:** Twenty-five minutes (journal, meditate, make bed)
2. **Bathroom:** Ten minutes (wash hands thoroughly, drink a fourteen-ounce glass of water, brush teeth)
3. **Office:** Two to six hours total (write/read for one to four hours and exercise for one to two hours. I either walk, or I do yoga. If I do yoga, I have a thirty-minute drive to/from the club.)

    ○ I listen to a book on my iPhone while walking or on my drive. I then write and edit my core values book for one to four hours.
    ○ Sometimes I read for one to three hours (especially if I'm teaching a volunteer class on "Great Books" or biographies/histories).
    ○ This takes me into the lunch hour. Regardless, I finish by midafternoon.

As you can see, I do not perform certain activities at certain times. Instead, I pair each habit with a preceding habit, a tip I read from BJ Fogg. Fogg recommends always anchoring a new habit to an old established habit in his book *Tiny Habits*.[23] (Find out more at TinyHabits.com.)

So within a few hours, I accomplish daily what I was never able to continuously do before. So simple. So easy.

How much do you think you would accomplish if you were doing this every day? How many books would you be able to read? How much could you write? How many projects would you complete in one year, ten years, or a lifetime?

Remember, I'm retired from my career. If I were not, I would have an entirely different schedule. During my preretirement life that was spent focusing on my core values, I went to my San Francisco office every day from 9 a.m. to 6 p.m., which are not long hours for an entrepreneur.

(If you're thinking *Where's breakfast?* I use intermittent fasting. I have my first meal at noon and dinner at 6 p.m. I am not recommending this for everyone, but it's what feels best for me.)

By the way, there is a very effective way to utilize stacked habits: the *Pomodoro Technique* (FrancescoCirillo.com)[24]

---

23 Fogg, BJ. *Tiny Habits: The Small Changes That Change Everything.* Boston: Houghton Mifflin Harcourt, 2020.

24 Cirillo, Francesco. "The Pomodoro Technique." FrancescoCirillo.com. Accessed August 13, 2020. https://francescocirillo.com/pages/pomodoro-technique.

instructs you to break your day into twenty-five-minute segments, each followed with a five-minute break. The twenty-five–minute segments allow you to perform "deep work" in an uninterrupted, highly focused way, typically on one thing. The short bursts help create highly productive (and high-quality) work. If you practice the *Pomodoro Technique,* over time, you'll accomplish great goals.

If you wish to live by your values and accomplish the goals associated with them, you will need discipline coupled with a system like the simple *Pomodoro Technique.*

Cirillo suggests refreshing yourself in this way during the five-minute breaks: "Breathe, meditate, grab a cup of coffee, go for a short walk or do something else relaxing (i.e., not work-related)."[25]

During most of the twenty-five-minute segments in my office time, I do not let emails interrupt me. If there is a pressing matter, I may dedicate one session exclusively to emails. Although I feel I am a disciplined person, I find that I need all the help I can get to maintain a daily productive schedule.

TWO OTHER BOOKS ON HABITS

There have been at least two other excellent books published

---

25   Cirillo, Francesco. "The Pomodoro Technique." FrancescoCirillo.com. Accessed August 13, 2020. https://francescocirillo.com/pages/pomodoro-technique.

about habits. *The Power of Habit* by Charles Duhigg[26] and *Atomic Habits* by James Clear (JamesClear.com).[27] Both emphasize the tremendous power of stacking habits versus using discipline or even goals. I will focus on Clear here. Clear tells us how to establish a habit and empower ourselves with simple habit statements.

Habits are created simply by doing the same thing every day. We simply start meditating, praying, journaling, walking, or reading for a specified amount of time on one day. Then we repeat it the next day. And so it goes. At some point, it becomes a habit, requiring no discipline and no further thought. Of course, we need to have a little discipline to get the ball rolling.

Clear states in *Atomic Habits*, "It's important to let your *values*, principles, and identity drive the loop rather than your results. The focus should always be on becoming that type of person, not getting a particular outcome…Goals are good for setting a direction, but systems are best for making progress…Winners and losers have the same *goals*" (all emphases added).[28]

So, the question becomes, "How do you build a new habit?"

26 Duhigg, Charles. *The Power of Habit: Why We Do What We Do in Life and Business.* New York: Random House, 2012.

27 Clear, James. *Atomic Habits.* New York: Avery, 2018.

28 Clear, James. *Atomic Habits.* New York: Avery, 2018.

You could go to JamesClear.com or buy *Atomic Habits* to find out. I did both. He broke down the process into five segments:

Start with an incredibly small habit.

Increase your habit in very small ways.

As you build up, break habits into chunks.

When you slip, get back on track quickly.

Be patient. Stick to a pace you can sustain.[29]

Once you learn the simple process, the next step is to yoke these two very powerful concepts together: core values and habits. Core values focus your efforts on those goals that are congruent with your values. Established habits then provide a powerful system for accomplishing those goals without needing much motivation or mental energy.

What I like best about habits are that they require neither thought nor motivation once they're set. We already have lots of habits. On average, 40 percent of what we do are habits.

---

29 Clear.

DO NOT STOP UNTIL IT'S A HABIT

There is one way that focusing on core values won't work. If you quit. I saw this firsthand during my many years of failure until my early thirties.

In the past ten years, when I taught core values to adults at a local college, I saw time and time again that some people would quit because they didn't have the discipline or willpower to see it through, to just put one foot ahead of the other day after day until it was a habit. (As the saying goes, "O ye of little faith.") They were unable to apply their core values and these concepts each day. That doesn't need to be you.

THOSE WHO SUCCEED VS. THOSE WHO FAIL

Let's talk about the difference between the two. They both have the same goals. Neither wants to do the necessary work to reach their goals, but those who succeed focus on their goals; those who fail focus on the hurdles they must overcome.

Those who succeed focus on the *prize*. Those who fail focus on the *price*.

The latter is unwilling to pay the price; this unwillingness is actually a habit, a very bad habit. If they can't break the habit, they will live a life of disappointment, disillusionment, and self-recrimination. That's a terrible price to pay, and they know it. (I knew I was paying that price when I was living in the San Franciscan skyrise, unhappy, having panic attacks.)

This may sound like a very judgmental opinion. It isn't. It's from an old study from *The Common Denominator of Success* (Albert E. N. Gray).[30] Yet, even if *this study* didn't exist, this has been my own personal experience. I was the failure, but later, I became the success. Why? Because I couldn't stomach failing all my life.

*The successful person has the **habit** of doing the things failures don't like to do. They don't like doing them either, necessarily. But their disliking is subordinated to the strength of their purpose. The subordination requires a purpose, a mission, a... clear sense of direction and value, a burning "yes!" inside that makes it possible to say "no" to other things.*

*It also requires independent will, the power to do something when you don't want to do it, to be a function of your **values** rather than a function of the impulse or desire of any given moment. [All emphases added.]*[31]

—STEPHEN R. COVEY, *THE 7 HABITS OF HIGHLY SUCCESSFUL PEOPLE*

30   Gray, Albert E. N. *The Common Denominator of Success.* Tremendous Life Books, 2008.

31   Covey, Stephen R. *The 7 Habits of Highly Effective People.* New York: Free Press, 1989.

WHY IS IT SO HARD TO STICK TO GOOD HABITS?

Habits are so important that I'm devoting half of a chapter to them. Clear gives us some insight as to why we give up on new habits so quickly:

> Have you ever set out with the goal of actually sticking to a new behavior...only to find yourself not doing it at all one week later? I know I have. Why is it so hard to form good habits? Why is it so difficult to make consistent change? How can we have the best intentions to become better, and yet still see so little progress? And most importantly, is there anything we can do about it?[32]

How do we balance our desire to make life-changing transformations with the need to build small, sustainable habits?

We recognize that good habits are created when we dream big but start small. As Clear states:

> What if you started thinking of your life goals, not as big, audacious things that you can only achieve when the time is right or when you have better resources or when you finally catch your big break...but instead as tiny, daily behaviors that are repeated until success becomes inevitable?...

---

32 Clear, James. "Why Is It So Hard to Stick to Good Habits." JamesClear.com. New York: Avery, 2018. Accessed August 13, 2020. https://jamesclear.com/why-is-it-so-hard-to-form-good-habits.

Daily habits—tiny routines that are repeatable—are what make big dreams a reality.[33]

Thank you, James. That's a good idea. I like focusing on habits that are consistent with my core values. As we've discussed, core values are closest to your heart, so it's much easier to do things that are congruent with those core values.

Maybe it's not a surprise that Clear does the same thing:

One of the solutions I've been trying out is to let my values drive my choices. That doesn't mean I ignore other aspects of my decision-making process. I simply add my core values into the mix.

For example, if I'm working on a problem in my business, rather than just asking, "Will this make money?" I can ask, "Is this in alignment with my values?" And then, "Will this make money?"

If I say no to either, then I look for another option. The idea behind this method is that if we live and work in alignment with our values, then we're more likely to live a life we are proud of rather than one we regret.[34]

---

33 Clear, James. "Why Is It So Hard to Stick to Good Habits." JamesClear.com. New York: Avery, 2018. Accessed August 13, 2020. https://jamesclear.com/why-is-it-so-hard-to-form-good-habits.

34 Clear, James. "Let Your Values Drive Your Choices." JamesClear.com. New York: Avery, 2018. Accessed August 13, 2020. https://jamesclear.com/why-is-it-so-hard-to-form-good-habits.

To start small and change your lifestyle, you will first need to evaluate your goals. See which of your goals are consistent with one or more of your ten to twenty internal core values. If you're following the system I have outlined for you, you are already committing to only acting on those goals, decisions, and actions consistent with your core values.

Even if your goals are good, they must be tested against your core values. For example, if you are writing a book and running several times a week, those are good goals, but are they congruent with one or more of your core values? If not, scratch them off the list right now. Knowing and acting on your core values has just saved you from wasting your time!

Setting small habits is a good idea. Combining those habits with core values is a better idea. It increases your chances for success in areas that matter most to you.

I hope you can see why discovering your core values before embarking on a productivity hack or a success-based system makes sense. Reverse the two, and you're wasting time. A lot of it.

Remember the productivity pyramid: purpose and values first, then goals, and tasks last. That's the key to success that Hyrum Smith and Covey taught around the world thirty years ago. It sure worked for them. It worked for me, too. All three of us realized our dreams: fulfillment, peace of mind, and financial freedom. That's a winning trifecta!

Every single qualification for success is acquired through habit. People form habits and habits form futures. If you do not deliberately form good habits, then unconsciously you will form bad ones. You are the kind of person you are because you have formed the habit of being that kind of person, and the only way you can change is through habit.[35]

—ALBERT GREY, *THE COMMON DENOMINATOR OF SUCCESS*

PART II: MAKING GOOD CHOICES WITHOUT (ONLY) USING WILLPOWER

Jari Roomer, the Founder of Personal Growth Lab (ThePersonalGrowthLab.com), wrote about the struggles of making the right choices. I am going to quote part of his article dealing with this issue because of its tie-in with core values:

> For many of us, there's a constant struggle with the self when it comes to making the "right" choices…Constantly, we're faced with the dilemma of instant vs delayed gratification. Yet, it is the quality of our decisions that determines the quality of our lives…
>
> **Why Willpower Doesn't Work**

---

35   Gray, Albert E. N. *The Common Denominator of Success.* Tremendous Life Books, 2008.

Tapping into your discipline and willpower is one way to overcome this struggle—and useful for picking the higher-quality option instead. The problem, however, is that our willpower is a finite resource that depletes during the day...

Link Your Identity to Your Choices

Whenever we're about to make a decision, we should ask ourselves the question, "Am I the type of person who picks X over Y?"...

In this case, picking the unhealthy donut over a healthy snack didn't match with the person that I believe myself to be—my identity. I think of myself as someone who values health, energy, and vitality...

Therefore, by confronting yourself with who you are if you make certain choices, you're much more likely to make better choices. The options that aren't in line with your identity simply become much less attractive.[36]

Thanks, Jari. Here's where your core values come into play with your identity. How would you think if you, like me, had health as a core value and you were in the above scenario?

---

36 Roomer, Jari. "How To Consistently Make Good Choices Without Tapping Into Your Willpower." Medium.com. Accessed August 13, 2020. https://medium.com/personal-growth-lab/how-to-consistently-make-good-choices-without-tapping-into-your-willpower.

Since my core value of health is defined as "I eat a balanced diet to have energy, skill, prevent cancer, and control weight," I don't have to access my willpower to say "no" to the donut.

This core value of health has become part of my persona. It is clear to me that eating donuts does not honor one of my eleven core values. It doesn't mean that I will never eat a donut. I think I have probably had three in the last year.

So, as opposed to fighting with my willpower, I can ask Jari's question: "Am I the kind of person who will choose to eat a donut over something healthier?" Asking identity-related questions is a good way to honor a core value.

CONCLUSION

I use both of these two tools—habits and avoiding dependence on my unreliable willpower—in combination with my core values to achieve results, and so can you! When tempted to do something unrelated to my values, I ask myself a question related to my self-image as a person who wants to succeed by following the internal core value that relates to that moment (see donut example, above). Sometimes it might be a bit more important than a donut—say, a life-changing decision like changing careers!

CHAPTER 8

THREE EFFECTIVE TOOLS YOU CAN USE WITH CORE VALUES

This chapter examines three efficient and powerful tools that are rarely used and understood: the Wheel of Life, the Matrix, and the Pareto Principle (I also provide a caution about the use of the Pareto Principle). They are simple and effective.

THE WHEEL OF LIFE

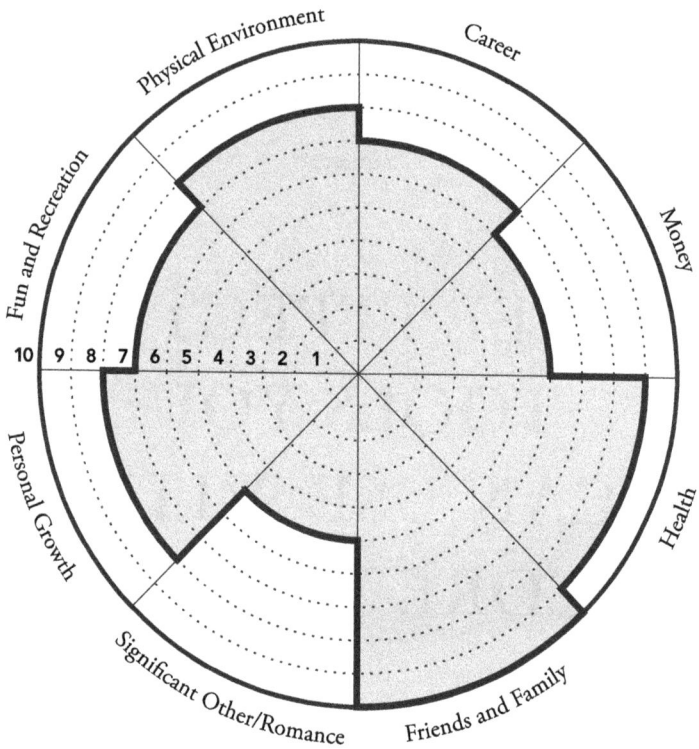

Here is a deceptively powerful tool you can use to measure your progress in honoring each of your core values. Let's assume you have these eight core values, and you've written your definitions for each. Each slice represents one of your eight core values. You take a snapshot of your progress every month. What we see above is your starting point recorded at the beginning. (This pie is divided into eight sections; when you use the Wheel of Life for yourself, cut it into as many pieces as needed to accommodate all of your core values.)

You rate each core value in terms of how much you are honoring it on a zero to ten scale, where zero means you are not honoring this core value at all. Every month, you can take these steps:

1. **Start with a blank Wheel of Life** (aka, start a new wheel with no dark lines).
2. **Give a ranking** to each of these eight core values in terms of how much you are honoring it in your daily decisions, setting goals, etc. Assume these are your rankings on day one of the first month:
   A. Career–7
   B. Money–6
   C. Health–9
   D. Friends and Family–10
   E. Significant Other/Romance–5
   F. Personal Growth–8
   G. Fun and Recreation–7
   H. Physical Environment–8

Note: This is an impressive chart. There are no values rated below a five, and six of the eight are rated seven or above.

3. **Draw a line** across each pie piece to visually represent your numerical rating for each core value.

4. Your goal is to have a big, smooth wheel (meaning all core values rated nine to ten). **Ask yourself two questions:**
   A. Assuming the dark lines represent a wheel, will this wheel roll?
   B. If it does roll, will it roll fast?

5. **Evaluate** your current status. Will your wheel roll? How fast? Will it be a rough or smooth ride? Specifically, what core value(s) need work? Identify and prioritize what values need the most attention.

6. **Improve.** You need to focus on the areas that need the most attention; in the scenario above, you would need to focus on the two lower-rated core values: money and significant other/romance. Here's a tip: from experience, I know you should focus on improving core values one at a time. People tend not to advance very quickly if they focus on all of the lower-rated core values at once.

7. **Grow.** Over time, you can get all of your core values in the eight-to-ten category. Your wheel will then roll better and faster. I have used this tool for twenty-six years. I have transferred the ratings to a spreadsheet so that I could compare my progress to the past. As I am writing this (2020), all eleven of my core values are rated eight to nine, and I'm a pretty tough judge of my progress. I rate no core value a ten. I always have room for improvement.

This tool is a powerful and effective visual representation of how you're doing in life. Use it.

THE MATRIX

Quadrant I	Quadrant II
Urgent and important	Not urgent but important
DO	**PLAN**
Quadrant III	Quadrant IV
Urgent but not important	Not urgent and not important
DELEGATE	**ELIMINATE**

What did Stephen R. Covey and Dwight D. Eisenhower use to focus their self-improvement efforts? The Matrix.

Here's how they prioritized their goals:[37]

- **Quadrant I**—crises, pressing problems, deadline-driven projects
- **Quadrant II**—prevention, relationship-building, new opportunities, planning, recreation
- **Quadrant III**—interruptions, some meetings, some mail and phone calls, pressing matters
- **Quadrant IV**—trivia, busy work, some mail and phone calls, time wasters, pleasant activities

If you are living a reckless life, you spend your time in Quad-

37 Covey, Stephen R. *The 7 Habits of Highly Effective People.* New York: Free Press, 1989.

rants III and IV. Covey: "People who spend time almost exclusively in Quadrants III and IV basically lead irresponsible lives."[38] If you manage your life by crisis, you will spend about 90 percent of your time in Quadrant I and the other 10 percent in Quadrant IV. Those people who are consistently living a life of purpose spend most of their time in Quadrant II.

"Effective people stay out of Quadrants III and IV because, urgent or not, they aren't important. They also shrink Quadrant I down to size by spending more time in Quadrant II,"[39] says Covey. Successful people are effective by focusing on Quadrant II—important but not urgent items. They do not let urgent items interrupt them and disrupt their flow.

Do you remember stacked habits and the *Pomodoro Technique*?[40] The entire point of using those was to do deep, uninterrupted work. So most of that work should be in Quadrant II. Some of the deadline-driven will remain in Quadrant I.

Quadrant II includes "building relationships, writing a personal mission statement, long-range planning, exercising, preventive maintenance, preparation—all those things we

---

38 Covey.

39 Covey.

40 Cirillo, Francesco. "The Pomodoro Technique." FrancescoCirillo.com. Accessed August 13, 2020. https://francescocirillo.com/pages/pomodoro-technique.

know we need to do, but somehow seldom get around to doing, because they aren't urgent." The results, Covey says, of living primarily in Quadrant II are "vision, perspective, balance, discipline, control, and few crises."[41]

Staying in Quadrant II brings the Pareto Principle into play—80 percent of the results flow out of 20 percent of the activities. But we must be disciplined about keeping our focus on Quadrant II because, Covey says, "It's almost impossible to say 'no' to the popularity of Quadrant III or to the pleasure of escape to Quadrant IV if you don't have a bigger 'yes' burning inside."[42]

So, where can we find that "'yes' burning inside"? By now, you should know that it comes from knowing your core values and operating upon them daily.

YOUR CORE VALUES TEND TO OPERATE IN QUADRANT II

Your core values tend to operate within one particular quadrant. Again, here are my eleven core values: spiritual, family, health, integrity, value-based life, community, freedom, accomplishment, learning and teaching, resoluteness, and renewal.

---

41 Covey, Stephen R. *The 7 Habits of Highly Effective People.* New York: Free Press, 1989.

42 Covey.

Do any of them have an *urgency* about them? No; so they can't be based in Quadrant I or Quadrant III.

Are any of my core values *not important*? Of course not.

All core values are *important* and *not urgent*. That puts all of them within Quadrant II.

As a matter of fact, people end up living in the urgent Quadrants I and III by *not* spending most of their time in Quadrant II. Why would anyone do that? They don't know any better, or they're not disciplined. So the question is:

Where do you spend your time?

The core-values approach will keep you operating in important but not urgent matters as much as possible in modern life. It will prune away those items that you must say "no" to.

Covey states: "What **one thing** [emphasis added] could you do in your personal and professional life that, if you did on a regular basis, would make a tremendous positive difference in your life? Quadrant II activities have that kind of impact. Our effectiveness takes quantum leaps when we do them."[43]

(This is all covered in more detail in Covey's book *The 7*

---

43 Covey, Stephen R. *The 7 Habits of Highly Effective People.* New York: Free Press, 1989.

Habits of Highly Effective People in chapter 3, "Put First Things First.")

THE PARETO PRINCIPLE

FIRST: A CAUTION

The Pareto Principle is very powerful. It is very reassuring to know that one can exert only 20 percent of the effort and still enjoy 80 percent of the benefits when learning a language, studying history, starting a new company, etc.

But here's the rub. How do you know with certainty which 20 percent to choose? If that was an easy decision, everyone would do it without hesitation. However, this principle is akin to saying, "If you buy one of these five houses on this street, you will enjoy great appreciation, far above the other four," or, "If you select the correct exercises, you can spend only 20 percent of the time and still lose weight and look great."

The issue is most of us don't know the productive 20 percent. Most of us don't know experts that we can absolutely count on to make these choices for us. Lastly, it often takes a long time, after much effort and guessing, to determine if we have selected the right 20 percent.

My wife and I bought a condo in a San Francisco high-rise several years ago. We did careful, thorough research. In the next few years, the price of condos in San Francisco plummeted. It took many years to recover the lost value.

Why did we fail even after careful, thorough research? One reason might be because we didn't know the correct 20 percent of real estate knowledge we needed to focus on. Or maybe it's what Nassim Nicholas Taleb calls a "black swan event," a largely unexpected event that's difficult to predict and leads to catastrophic consequences.[44]

Following your core values is another matter entirely. We know how to find them. This book explains that. Following core values is like using a supercharged Pareto Principle. It's likely to work every time. After all, you are only doing things that are closest to your heart, and you can choose those things based on your inherent desires and values.

When I finally tried this approach in 1993, I simply hoped it was true. (I had discovered long before then that refusing to believe new things and take calculated risks would not get me anywhere.)

In a few years, I saw that a values-based approach worked wonders in my life.

In summary, the Pareto Principle is an efficiency tool that

44 Taleb, Nassim Nicholas. *The Black Swan: The Impact of the Highly Improbable.* New York: Random House, 2007.

promises many benefits. However, discovering and following one's core values means you are doing things that give you immense pleasure since they honor deeply held values, things that are closest to your heart. (It is remarkable to me that within each of us, there are ten to twenty core values that distinguish us from all other individuals.)

When we follow our core values, often, we don't need to wait long for the rewards. With only a little diligence, we will see them, resulting in a full and rich life.

So, is the Pareto Principle or core values "better"? Here's my question: why can't you do both? They really aren't competitive systems. As a matter of fact, following your core values does not compete with any goal-achievement system.

SUMMARY OF TOOLS

In this chapter we discussed three efficiency tools. The Wheel of Life will give you a regular way to measure your progress in living consistently with your core values. The Matrix provides another visual tool to keep your focus where it should be: on things that provide "vision, perspective, balance, discipline, control, and few crises."[45] Lastly, use of the Pareto Principle gives you high leverage in achieving your goals. But how do you know which 20 percent to focus on? That's

---

45   Covey, Stephen R. *The 7 Habits of Highly Effective People.* New York: Free Press, 1989.

easy: focus *only* on those goals that are consistent with your core values.

CHAPTER 9

—

HOW TO FIND
YOUR "WHY"

You may have noticed we've ignored what some feel is the true foundation of our productivity pyramid—finding your purpose (or your "why"). While this book is not primarily about finding your purpose, this important motivator cannot be ignored.

If you have examined your core values, you should be better prepared to consider your purpose. Let's add your purpose beneath core values on our productivity pyramid.

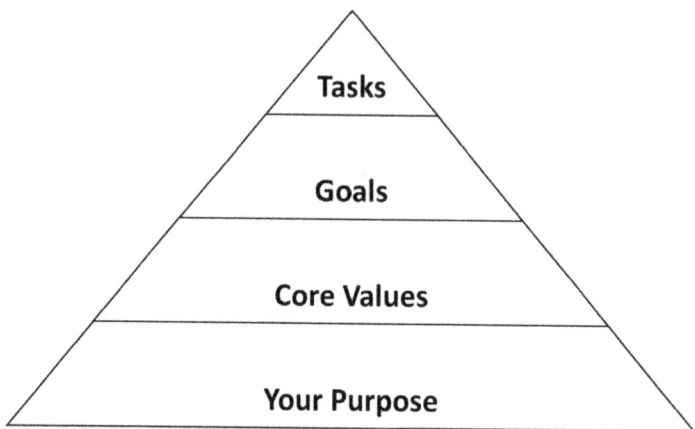

Forget about willpower. It's time for why-power. Your choices are only meaningful when you connect them to your desires and dreams. The wisest and most motivating choices are the ones aligned with that which you identify as your purpose, your core self, and your highest values. You've got to want something, and know why you want it, or you'll end up giving up too easily.[46]

—DARREN HARDY

HOW DO YOU FIND YOUR "WHY"? READ—A LOT

Finding your "why" can be difficult, very difficult.

I have a solution: read (a lot).

I know from experience.

---

46 Hardy, Darren, *The Compound Effect*. Philadelphia: Vanguard Press, 2010.

It was very difficult for me to find my purpose. I kept reading how important it was but didn't quite know where to start. More reading, thinking, and prayer came in.

I've often thought that after finishing their schooling, most people make an unconscious choice. They either choose to continue learning, or they've had enough and focus on entertainment or fun. I estimate that 80–90 percent choose the latter. These folks stop learning, or, to be more accurate, they stop learning much, which means they also stop growing much. These are the folks you meet at high school and college reunions who you notice haven't changed much since school. (I hope no one ever tells me that.)

These folks watch a lot of TV and focus primarily on entertaining. They spend much of their time on social media and politics. Their vacations are not learning experiences. They're more apt to go somewhere where they can have fun. (To understand how many people fall into this camp, look at the ads for vacation spots: the advertisement is mostly about food and fun.)

These folks don't read much. They know little of literature, history, art, philosophy, or success books. In my career as an entrepreneur, I rarely met people who read frequently. Most only knew *their* business and entertainment. Even their hobbies rarely included much learning. What a small box in which to live your life.

Some may change their mind much later, after their schooling or, like me, later in their career, and start learning. As I look back, I'm reasonably certain I did not begin focusing on learning and reading until I was in my late thirties.

Why does reading matter so much? Simply put: To succeed, you must overcome obstacles. To overcome obstacles, you must grow. To grow, you must learn. To learn much, you must read much.

Of course, there are other ways to learn. You can learn in your career, relationships, and hobbies. But you learn far more from reading. It allows one to learn how others have succeeded (and failed) versus learning purely from your own experience. You also learn about ways others have used to succeed and avoid failure. When you read (serious) books, you change, you grow, you become a different person. I specifically mean literature, biographies, history books, books on philosophy, and self-help books. I am not talking about romance, sci-fi, or other entertainment-only books.

I would be very selective with self-help books and blogs. I read some of them, but my primary focus is on the four other book categories (literature, biographies, history, and philosophy). This means you *won't* be focusing on current bestsellers.

I'm talking about Great Books and specifically the *New*

Lifetime Reading Plan by Fadiman and Major.[47] Excellent literature. The best. These are the books written by great authors. Those are the ones that I learned from, and so can you.

This is a highly subjective subject. Literature is a very loose term without an objective definition. Anything can be included or excluded. So allow me to try to be more specific: I'm talking about high-quality writing. The Encyclopedia Britannica classified this type of literature as "the best expression of the best thought reduced to writing."[48]

Nothing that I can write satisfies. We'll just have to leave it there. My own opinion would exclude most books. I refer you to the Fadiman and Major book listed above; there are 233 books listed in two separate lists in my copy. For most folks, finishing that list might take a lifetime. There are many fine books that do not make this cut. So let's include the finest, best-reviewed of the rest, a very subjective approach.

This should really be a subject for a book. And it actually is for a number of books. One of my favorites is *How to Read a Book* (Adler and Van Doren).[49] Its subtitle is *The Classic*

---

47 Fadiman, Clifton, and John S. Major. *The New Lifetime Reading Plan: The Classic Guide to World Literature, Revised and Expanded.* 4th ed. New York: HarperPerennial, 1997.

48 *The Encyclopædia Britannica*, 11th ed. (1911), s.v. "Literature." (Chicago: Horace Everett Hooper), vol 16:12.

49 Adler, Mortimer J., and Charles Van Doren. *How to Read a Book: The Classic Guide to Intelligent Reading.* New York: Simon & Schuster, 1972.

Guide to Intelligent Reading. It was originally published in 1940 and is considered a classic.

A reader lives a thousand lives before he dies. The man who never reads lives only one.[50]

—GEORGE R. R. MARTIN, AUTHOR, SCREENWRITER, AND
PRODUCER (BEST KNOWN FOR *GAME OF THRONES*)

It is far better to read about failure than experience it. If you don't read excellent literature, you are limiting your learning to your own experience.

FINDING MY "WHY" CHANGED EVERYTHING

When I developed a big-enough "why," everything changed. I started hanging around other well-read folks. I read more and studied more. I began a library of 1,700 books, including many books on success. I even read Aristotle's book *Nicomachean Ethics*[51] (this may be the best success book ever written, and it was written over two thousand years ago!).

My "why" evolved over time. Sometimes I had to expand my "why" or even find a different one. I also found that when someone has a big "why," they begin to look at others differently. They can see that most lack focus and drive, and their

---

50   Martin, George R. R. *A Dance with Dragons*. New York: Bantam Books, 2011

51   Aristotle. *The Nicomachean Ethics*. Translated by David Ross. Oxford: Oxford University Press, 2009.

conversations lack purpose. On the other hand, when you meet others who know their "why," they're generally interesting to converse with and be around. They're alive! You both learn from each other. It is easy—very easy—to identify the few people who have purpose.

HOW TO FOSTER NEW DYNAMIC RELATIONSHIPS

In 2014, my wife and I went on a cruise traveling around the United Kingdom. We met a gentleman and his wife who always seemed to be with interesting, dynamic folks. I asked the couple if they had come with a group of friends. They came alone.

I asked how he was always with interesting people.

First, he told me they never dined on the ship with only one other couple. He always asked to be seated with at least *two* couples.

Second, they also did not go on the planned ship excursions. They went on private excursions with a few other couples they had met. He felt that the smaller groups rather than the much larger cruise tours brought his group closer together. (These private tours were also much cheaper.)

Why did he do those two things? He said that he and his wife increased their odds of meeting an interesting, dynamic couple.

Well, it worked for him and his wife and, later, for my wife and me. What a difference it's made since then.

YOUR "WHY" CAN ALSO BE CALLED YOUR "DEFINITE MAJOR PURPOSE"

Knowing others is intelligence; knowing yourself is true wisdom.

Mastering others is strength; mastering yourself is true power.[52]

—LAO-TZU, CHINESE PHILOSOPHER, FROM *TAO TE CHING*

Without a major purpose, you are drifting toward certain failure.[53]

—THE NAPOLEON HILL FOUNDATION

A definite major purpose may only be one sentence or a few words for you. Refining such a significant aspect of your life is always tougher than wrestling with a single core value or two. It will rarely be done on the first effort. It's like a sculpture that will need to be reworked many times before you get it right. Even then, it will probably evolve as you grow and change.

If you have completed your core values, you are headed in the right direction. If you have not, then pause before finding your "why," your definite major purpose. Wait until you've discovered your core values; these tell you who you are. It is crucial to know your core values first, before you try to find your "why" (aka, your definite major purpose).

---

52   Lao-tzu. "33." *Tao Te Ching*. Translated by Stephen Mitchell. New York: HarperCollins, 1988.

53   "Thought for the Day, August 16th, 2020." The Napoleon Hill Foundation. https://www.naphill.org/tftd/thought_for_the_day_08-16-20/.

After years of work, here is my "why" (or definite major purpose) in one sentence:

I give to others while living a morally and spiritually upright life in concert with my values and goals.

This book is an example of that statement. (You will notice that "money" was not present in my "why." I am not against making money, but that is not my purpose in general or for writing this book specifically.)

This simple "why," or my definite major purpose, has changed my life and given me fulfillment, peace of mind, and financial independence. Along with deepening my spiritual life, meeting my wife, and naming my core values, finding my "why" was one of the most important things I ever did.

For further consideration on finding your "why" or your definite major purpose, there are many good blogs and books on this subject, such as *Find Your Why: A Practical Guide for Discovering Purpose for You and Your Team* by Simon Sinek, David Mead, and Peter Docker.[54] Another one of my favorites is *Finding Your Purpose* by Barbara J. Braham.[55]

---

54 Sinek, Simon, David Mead, and Peter Docker. *Find Your Why: A Practical Guide for Discovering Purpose for You and Your Team*. New York: Portfolio/Penguin, 2017.

55 Braham, Barbara J. *Finding Your Purpose: A Guide to Personal Fulfillment*. Crisp Publications Incorporated, 1991.

This is a workbook, and it worked like magic for me. (I used the 1991 edition.)

WHY YOU SHOULD NOT FOLLOW YOUR PASSION

"Follow your passion, and you'll never work a day in your life!"

That sounds like wisdom, but it's bad advice. There are many reasons. Here are a few:

- **You may be passionate about something that doesn't earn a good living.** Unless earning a good living doesn't matter to you, following your passion may not lead toward fulfillment.
- **Passion comes and goes.** Passion for many things (and people) often changes over time. Sometimes boredom sets in. Sometimes you get involved with the wrong people. Conversely, sometimes passion can grow when the situation and people are better than your first thought. You simply can't predict passion.
- **What sounds terrific at first sometimes turns out to be a drag when you become immersed in the details.** This is quite common. Have you ever done something that sounded exciting, but it resulted in pure tedium?
- **Often your skills may not match what is necessary and even essential to succeed in the area of your passion.**
- **You may not have passion and expertise in the same thing.** Silicon Valley investor Ben Horowitz gave a speech

to Columbia's graduating class in 2015 and provided four reasons why recent college grads shouldn't follow their passions (two of them repeat my points above):[56]

- *Passions are hard to prioritize. Are you more passionate about math, or engineering? History, or literature? "On the other hand, what are you good at? That's a much easier thing to figure out," he said.*
- *Passions change. "What you're passionate about at twenty-one is not necessarily what you're gonna be passionate about at forty."*
- *You may not be good at it. "Has anybody ever watched American Idol?" he asked. "Just because you love singing doesn't mean you should be a professional singer."*
- *It's self-centered. He explained that over time, people learn that what they take out of the world is much less important than what they leave behind.*
- *His advice? "Find that thing you're great at. Put that into the world. Contribute to others. Help the world be better."*

- Author and professor at Georgetown University Cal Newport published a book titled *So Good They Can't Ignore You*.[57] "It argued that 'follow your passion' was bad career advice. I didn't claim that passion was a problem, but instead argued that it was too simplistic to assume that

---

56 Rosoff, Matt. "Why One of Silicon Valley's Top Investors Says 'Don't Follow Your Passion.'" *Business Insider*. May 29, 2015.

57 Newport, Cal. *So Good They Can't Ignore You: Why Skills Trump Passion in the Quest for Work You Love*. New York: Grand Central Publishing, 2012.

the key to career satisfaction was as easy as matching your job to a pre-existing inclination. For many people, this slogan might actually *impede* their progress down the more complicated path that leads to true satisfaction."[58]

Setting out to find passion can be a failure, but finding passion or satisfaction in your work later can be wonderful. In my career, I found that when I was successful, I would often feel passion. When I was *very* successful, passion almost certainly came along for the ride. For me and many others, passion follows success, not the other way around.

So instead of passion, what should you look for?

Look for a career that will honor your core values. If you have discovered your core values using the process outlined earlier in this book, then you know that to find ultimate fulfillment, you need to make every decision based upon whether or not it is congruent or consistent with one or more of your core values. These values are closest to your heart and inherent within you. Doesn't it make sense to only do those things that are closest to your heart?

Once you start doing that, you'll note that decision-making

---

58   Newport, Cal. "Ancient Complications to Modern Career Advice." *Study Hacks* (blog). CalNewport.com. June 13, 2020. https://www.calnewport.com/blog/2020/06/13/ancient-complications-to-modern-career-advice/.

will be easier and hence so will life. Over time, you will find, as I did, that such a life leads to fulfillment and peace of mind.

Let me be specific. If I was once again looking for work, I would not accept any position where I felt that I could not honor my core values or one that would directly conflict with them: spiritual, family, health, integrity, value-based life, community, freedom, accomplishment, learning and teaching, resoluteness, and renewal.

Not all core values might apply, but I certainly would require high integrity, a strong sense of community, and a place where I could learn (and eventually teach). I would not accept any position that would jeopardize my family nor one that was not value focused. I might reject long hours and tight control since that could conflict with my family and freedom core values. Perhaps it would be best if I stayed in the entrepreneurial realm, where, as my own boss, I could control the environment and structure to a greater extent.

In late 2019, in a conversation with someone whom I consider to be the most important person in teaching this approach, I asked Hyrum Smith if he thought that, in general, following your core values often leads to financial independence. He said that he believed it did—it did for him (it did for me, too). Of course, there are so many variables when it comes to financial freedom that it cannot be promised.

WAIT. AREN'T PASSION AND CORE VALUES THE SAME THING?

No, passion and core values are not equivalent, but they are closely related in one critical way. Let's look at the definition of core values one more time:

Deeply rooted fundamental beliefs. Guides that dictate your behavior and actions. The foundations of what is driving your decisions. Ingrained principles that help you declare who you are and what you stand for.[59]

—DAWN BARCLAY

Since these ten to twenty values are inherent within you, have been so since before you became an adult, don't seem to change much, and are closest to your heart, doesn't it make sense that you may feel strongly about them? You will likely even be *passionate* about them. I certainly experienced passion as I started living according to my core values, and you will likely experience it as well.

So therefore, finding your core values could be a good first step to finding your true passion. Some folks do find short-term gratification that they call "passion." But without any idea what their core values are, that "passion" may be short-lived. That "passion" is for some work or career that they only currently think they truly care about.

---

59   Barclay, Dawn. "Core Values." *Living Moxie.* Accessed August 13, 2020. https://dawnbarclay.com/core-values/.

This is not trivial. We're talking about the rest of your life, perhaps forty or more years. You don't get a do-over!

Remember Clint Eastwood's cautionary question: "Ask yourself one question: 'Do I feel lucky?'" (You probably don't feel lucky enough to bet forty or more years of your life on pursuing something that doesn't lead to true and lasting fulfillment.)

FINAL THOUGHTS ON PASSION

Now that you've discovered your "why," or your definite major purpose, you've built a good foundation: you know your purpose. Very few people have ever taken this step. Most have no idea what their purpose is.

Also in this chapter, we took a look at why following your passion may not be a good idea. If instead, you do things that honor your core values, you will be focusing on those things that are closest to your heart, and you are more likely to find long-lasting fulfillment, peace of mind, and financial independence. Further, you are more likely to find your true passion by first starting with your core values rather than by chasing what feels good in the moment.

CHAPTER 10

SELF-KNOWLEDGE

THE KEY TO CHOOSING
YOUR ESSENTIAL GOALS

"Experts" talk a lot about accomplishing goals.

They tell you how to maximize your time. They may even tell you how to set goals, but do they help you *select* goals?

I read their blogs and books and listen to their audios, but the experts simply cannot help you pick the right goals for you. Why will no one help with this crucial aspect of life? Read on.

In this chapter, we look at the importance of self-knowledge and how it enables you to find the right goals for your life. Already, you know that discovering your core values is invaluable self-knowledge. Once you couple that with learning which goals are essential in your life, you have a good start on a fulfilled and happy life. I close this chapter with the question "What is essential in your life?"

KNOW THYSELF

There is strong scientific evidence that people who know themselves and how others see them are happier. They make smarter decisions. They have better personal and professional relationships. They raise more mature children. They're smarter, superior students who choose better careers. They're more creative, more confident, and better communicators. They're less aggressive and less likely to lie, cheat, and steal. They're better performers at work who get more promotions. They're more effective leaders with more enthusiastic employees. They even lead more profitable companies.[60]

—DR. TASHA EURICH, *INSIGHT*, LEADERSHIP
EXPERT, SPEAKER, AND AUTHOR

Fortunately, in the rest of her book *Insight*, Dr. Eurich reveals that self-awareness is a surprisingly developable skill. Integrating hundreds of studies with her own research and work in the Fortune 500 world, she shows us what it really takes to better understand ourselves on the inside.

If you've read this far, you now know how to increase your

---

60 Eurich, Tasha. *Insight: Why We're Not as Self-Aware as We Think, and How Seeing Ourselves Clearly Helps Us Succeed at Work and in Life.* New York: Currency, 2017.

self-awareness: you start by discovering your ten to twenty internal core values. This is who you are. (Isn't it amazing how many different writers and philosophers all make this same or similar point?)

The origin of "know thyself" has been attributed to many philosophers, even before Socrates, who expounded on this by saying, "The unexamined life is not worth living."[61] The saying was further used by Aeschylus, Plato, Thomas Hobbes, Alexander Pope, Benjamin Franklin, Jean-Jacques Rosseau, Ralph Waldo Emerson, and Samuel Coleridge. So, if we decide to use this same philosophy, we're in good company.

I can't think of a better way to know thyself or increase your self-awareness than by discovering your core values and applying them to every part of your life: your goals, your decisions, and your actions.

REMEMBER: YOU WILL SAVE MUCH TIME AND EFFORT BY FIRST UNDERSTANDING YOUR CORE VALUES

Before we dive into selecting your essential goals, I'd like to review just how much time starting with your core values really saves.

Before aligning your goals with your core values, let's assume

61 Plato. *The Apology of Socrates.*

all of your thousands of goals, decisions, and actions are spread among the entire list of values. I have identified over 400 personal values, but the average person only has ten to twenty of those. That's a maximum of 5 percent of all personal values.

So, by focusing on your ten to twenty core values, you would be eliminating most values, goals, decisions, and actions from your life. That also means you would eliminate most of the blogs, books, articles, and podcasts, too.

As you eliminate most of the clutter, your life becomes simpler. Decisions are easier to make. You spend much less time and effort on decisions, and you become far more satisfied with how you spend your time.

This sounds obvious, but so many people ignore it. They keep writing about how you can *accomplish* goals (without telling you how to choose them), which productivity hacks to use, how to build productive habits, which books and blogs to read, which podcasts to listen to, etc.

That advice may not be helpful, or it may be irrelevant, depending on your core values. You will not reach fulfillment or happiness by getting up early, taking cold showers, setting habits, reading and studying, meditating, giving gratitude, or getting mentors. You will find happiness by accomplishing goals that align with your core values.

Many of those productivity hacks will not work for you because the experts leave out a key ingredient: the selection of goals that are consistent with your core values. The experts assume you know your goals (or how to find them).

Yes—I use many of those productivity hacks and suggestions, but they did little good for me before I took the key step:

Carefully selecting *my* goals.

"Cheshire Cat," asked Alice, "would you tell me, please, which way I ought to go from here?" "That depends a good deal on where you want to go," said the Cat. "I don't much care where," said Alice. "Then it doesn't matter which way you go," said the Cat.[62]

—LEWIS CARROLL

ONLY YOU CAN CHOOSE THE RIGHT GOALS FOR YOU

You are a unique person living in a specific place with unique work, family, and friends. Your life is unique; it is not like mine nor is it like those of your friends and acquaintances. All the hacks and systems in the world that help you be efficient and effective won't help if the wrong goals are picked.

---

62 Carroll, Lewis. *Alice's Adventures in Wonderland*. London: MacMillan & Co., Limited, 1912.

The measure of intelligence is the ability to change.

—UNKNOWN

Everything I read is based on the assumption you know how to select the best goals for you. Rarely does anyone give any help in telling you how to find out what goals are best for you.

Nobody calls them on it, but you know why they don't tell you how to find your goals? Because they can't. They have no idea what goals are best for you. You're on your own.

The highest level of mastery is simplicity. Most information is irrelevant and most effort is wasted, but only the expert knows what to ignore.[63]

—JAMES CLEAR, JAMESCLEAR.COM, *ATOMIC HABITS*

So how can you decide what goals are right for you? How do you decide what your priorities are? How do you decide what to say "no" to? How do you decide what you're going to do today, or this week, or this year?

Here is what's even more ominous to consider: what happens if you pick the wrong goals?

That's where I was for the first thirty-two years of my career.

---

63   Clear, James. "3-2-1: On the highest level of mastery, being a positive force, and living a meaningful life." *The 3-2-1 Newsletter*, November 21, 2019. https://jamesclear.com/3-2-1/november-21-2019.

I had good jobs with good companies, but I had no specific goals I believed in and reviewed daily. Result: I was a failure. Luckily, all that changed in year thirty-three of my career!

Steve Jobs talked about the value of knowing what to say "no" to, but how can you know when to say "no" if you don't know how to pick your goals?

The difference between successful people and really success-ful people is that really successful people say no to almost everything.[64]

—WARREN BUFFETT

Buffet, Steve Jobs, and others all seem to think that you know how to select the best goals for yourself. Yet you don't want to just hope that you're lucky. (When luck is involved, remember Clint Eastwood as Dirty Harry.)

We intuitively know there must be a way. You've already read about the starting place in this book: once you know your ten to twenty internal core values, you can then select those goals that are consistent with them. Every day. You will finally have the answer to the question: how do you pick your goals?

Once you've discovered your core values, then, with

64 Haden, Jeff. "Warren Buffett Says 1 Thing Separates Successful People From All the Rest (and Leads to Living a Fulfilling and Rewarding Life)." *Inc.com*, December 11, 2018. https://www.inc.com/jeff-haden/warren-buffet-says-1-thing-separates-successful-people-from-all-rest-and-leads-to-living-a-fulfilling-rewarding-life.html.

confidence, you can use your favorite goals-based or productivity-hack system to focus on those goals that matter to you, deeply. You can rest easy knowing that down the road, accomplishing those goals will likely result in the promise that Hyrum Smith made: fulfillment and inner peace!

If you feel lucky, you can use some system other than choosing your core values first, but remember: the stakes are high. Further, there is a possibility that if you continue down the wrong path, you will fall prey to what is known as "the sunk-cost effect." Christopher Olivola, an assistant professor of marketing at Carnegie Mellon's Tepper School of Business and author of a paper on the effect in the journal *Psychological Science,* described this as "the general tendency for people to continue an endeavor, or continue consuming or pursuing an option if they've invested time or money or some resource in it."[65] I know that feeling.

Consider what may happen if you've set your goals incorrectly:[66]

> And one of the interesting things about success is that we think we know what it means…And the thing about a successful life is that a lot of the time, our ideas of what it

---

65 Ducharme, Jamie. "The Sunk Cost Fallacy Is Ruining Your Decisions. Here's How." *Time,* July 26, 2018.

66 Botton, Alain de. "A Kinder, Gentler Philosophy of Success." Talk presented at a TED Conference, July 2009. https://www.ted.com/talks/alain_de_botton_a_kinder_gentler_philosophy_of_success/transcript?language=en.

would mean to live successfully are not our own. They're sucked in from other people...And we also suck in messages from everything from the television to advertising to marketing, etcetera...So what I want to argue for is not that we should give up on our ideas of success, but that we should make sure that they are our own...**Because it's bad enough not getting what you want, but it's even worse to have an idea of what it is you want, and find out, at the end of the journey, that it isn't, in fact, what you wanted all along.**

—ALAIN DE BOTTON, PHILOSOPHER AND AUTHOR OF *THE PLEASURES AND SORROWS OF WORK* (EMPHASIS ADDED)

Robert Greene, in *Mastery*, adds this about selecting the wrong goals:

A false path in life is generally something we are attracted to for the wrong reasons—money, fame, attention, and so on...Because the field we choose does not correspond with our deepest inclinations, we rarely find the fulfillment that we crave. Our work suffers for this, and the attention we may have gotten in the beginning starts to fade—a painful process.[67]

If we glean from these thinkers, it's clear that choosing the wrong goals sure doesn't sound good. Yet, I don't see the system of choosing the right goals taught anywhere. Why was

67   Greene, Robert. *Mastery*. New York: Viking, 2012.

this knowledge lost? When Covey and Hyrum Smith retired, no one else stepped into the void. With the information in your hand, you no longer need to worry. You know now how to choose the right goals.

START WITH THE ESSENTIALS

From Greg McKeown's *Essentialism*:

> A woman named Cynthia once told me a story…
>
> Twelve-year-old Cynthia and her father had been planning the "date" for months. They had a whole itinerary planned down to the minute: she would attend the last hour of his presentation, and then meet him at the back of the room at about four-thirty and leave quickly before everyone tried to talk to him.
>
> [An old friend and business associate invited Cynthia and her father to dinner. Her father politely turned the invitation down.]
>
> "Cynthia and I have a special date planned, don't we?" He winked at Cynthia and grabbed her hand and they ran out of the door and continued with what was an unforgettable night in San Francisco.
>
> Cynthia's father…was Stephen R. Covey (author of *The*

Seven Habits of Highly Effective People) who had passed away only weeks before Cynthia told me this story.

His simple decision "Bonded him to me forever because I knew what mattered most to him was me!" she said.

Stephen R. Covey…was an Essentialist.[68]

Thank you, Greg, for both the quote and the great book.

LASTLY, PUTTING IT ALL TOGETHER

Knowing which goals, decisions, and actions are essential for a fulfilled life and which are nonessential is important. Further, knowing which of these things is closest to your heart is helpful. That is the very essence of your core values. It helps you find what is essential in your life. Yoking self-knowledge and essentialism to your core values is a winner!

How do you choose your goals based upon your values? Chapter 6 shows you how I did it after I retired in 2004. I started with a blank slate.

It's different if you're working. You already have plenty of responsibilities, many of which are somewhat mandatory. You don't have much unassigned time every day. You can't

---

68 McKeown, Greg. *Essentialism: The Disciplined Pursuit of Less*. New York: Crown Business, 2014.

do everything that appeals to you. But you can change some of the things that you do if they are not consistent with your core values. You can say "no" to new activities that are inconsistent with your core values and start choosing the activities that *are* consistent with your core values.

Reread the section of chapter 4 that deals with my eleven core values. You will notice that my description of each core value identifies or suggests many activities that I could undertake to honor my values while still in a career. For example, I chose aerobics, walking, and yoga as activities I could perform while still in my career to align with my core value of health. The rest of the activities I chose and the goals I set that align with my core values are as follows: philanthropy (community and spiritual core values); aerobics, walking, and yoga (health); investment program (freedom); setting lifetime goals (accomplishment); taking and teaching classes, listening to books and classes on my iPhone while walking (learning and teaching); and nature, music, and the arts (renewal). Most of these I could accomplish while still working.

So for you, do the same. Use your creativity to come up with activities and goals that align with your core values. Further, ensure that these goals and activities are realistic based on your current life, family obligations, and career.

IN SUMMARY

So there you have it: a blueprint for selecting qualified activities that are consistent with your core values. For me, it was trial and error. Over time, however, it worked wonderfully. Don't become someone who accomplishes goals that are not congruent with your core values. How can that be fulfilling? Accomplishing goals that do not stem from your core values will leave you frustrated and without the promise of peace.

CHAPTER 11

———

WAS ARISTOTLE RIGHT ABOUT HAPPINESS?

I taught a class for adults at a local college on core values. I asked how many people liked philosophy. Few hands were raised.

Then I said this: "Allow me to offer this definition of philosophy: philosophy is the focus on the proper relationship of man to man, man to the earth, and man to God. Now how many are interested?"

Most hands shot up.

So be patient with me as we now turn to philosophy. Let's

look at Aristotle, first. Some feel that Aristotle's book *Nicomachean Ethics*[69] is the best book ever written on the subject of happiness.

Next, we look at the case for reading philosophy made by the guy who may have done more than anyone to popularize philosophy today: Ryan Holiday. He focuses on what was once a little-known branch of philosophy: Stoicism. He makes a strong case for adopting the tenets of this philosophy.

ARISTOTLE AND HAPPINESS

The ideas of the Greek philosopher Aristotle can still help us create better lives and communities. Dr. Edith Hall, a professor of classics at King's College London, recently wrote *Aristotle's Way: How Ancient Wisdom Can Change Your Life.*[70] She wrote an essay for the *Wall Street Journal* in 2019 that explains many of the premises from the book. It states in part:

> Aristotle's ethical system—as described in his major treatises, the *Nicomachean Ethics* and the *Eudemian Ethics*—revolves around the idea that the goal of human life is happiness…For him, happiness was an internal state of mind…

---

69 Aristotle. *The Nicomachean Ethics.* Translated by David Ross. Oxford: Oxford University Press, 2009.

70 Hall, Edith. *Aristotle's Way: How Ancient Wisdom Can Change Your Life.* New York: Penguin Press, 2019.

Real happiness, Aristotle believed, comes from a continuous effort to become the best possible version of yourself. Like his teacher Plato and Plato's own teacher, he subscribed to the ancient proverb engraved over the oracle at Delphi: Know thyself...

Aristotle does not teach, for instance, that anger is a vice and patience a virtue. Rather, he believes that when we feel anger in the right amount, at the right time and toward the right people, it is virtuous. Without it, we wouldn't stand up for ourselves or for important principles. Failing to feel anger when we are wronged is a vice, but then so is excessive, misplaced or gratuitous anger...

Good Aristotelians acknowledge both their best and their worst moral characteristics and work continuously at self-improvement. They try to develop habits of **generosity, honesty, responsibility, integrity, fairness, kindness and good humor.** [Emphasis added.][71]

Note the emboldened words **generosity, honesty, responsibility, integrity, fairness, kindness, and good humor.** These are mentioned by Dr. Hall (and extrapolated from Aristotle's philosophy) as "habits," but they can also be core values. Or

---

71 Hall, Edith. "Aristotle's Pursuit of Happiness: The Ideas of the Greek Philosopher Can Still Help Us Create Better Lives and Communities." *Wall Street Journal*, January 31, 2019. https://www.wsj.com/articles/aristotles-pursuit-of-happiness-11548950094.

they can be part of larger core values. "Honesty" may be viewed as part of "integrity," for instance.

If you can turn a core value into a habit, you are on your way to living a successful and purposeful life. If you honor them in your daily decisions, actions, and goals, you will be on your way to realizing fulfillment and peace of mind. These are other words for happiness.

In my life, it didn't take long to find that focusing on my core values worked. I could see that my life had changed dramatically. (I wonder what those chaps sitting around the Lyceum in Athens would have thought?)

There's something inside you that knows when you're in the center, that knows when you're on the beam or off the beam. And if you get off the beam to earn money, you've lost your life. And if you stay in the center and don't get any money, you still have your bliss.[72]

—JOSEPH CAMPBELL, *THE POWER OF MYTH*

WHY EVERYONE SHOULD BECOME A PHILOSOPHER

When I was in college, I studied engineering, physics, and mathematics. I had wanted a challenge and got it in spades.

---

72 Campbell, Joseph, with Bill Moyers. *The Power of Myth*. New York: Anchor Books, 1991.

That was a big mistake. After I graduated, I spent my career in marketing.

I did enjoy taking a few classes on philosophy. I liked it so much that I considered becoming a philosopher, but it's difficult to land a job in that field. I have yet to meet a professional philosopher.

Philosophy has been given a bad rap. It helps us become more introspective. That is a precursor to most personal change. What could be more important than trying to understand what our relationship should be to other people, our God, and our planet? What is more crucial than understanding how to live?

Ryan Holiday wrote a blog post entitled "Why You Should Study Philosophy," which I've included in part below.

> If philosophy is anything, it's an answer to that question about how to live. "Would you really know what philosophy offers to humanity?" Seneca asks in his *Moral Letters*, "Philosophy offers counsel." It gives us advice. It consoles us. It explains…

> That's what studying philosophy—reading and meditating on the wisdom of great minds—does. It strengthens our ability to remain steady in the chaos and rush of life. It takes the crooked, confusing, and overwhelming

nature of external events and makes them orderly. And that, Epictetus said, is freedom.[73]

Thank you, Ryan Holiday. After reading this blog and thinking about the importance of doing the right thing, we are left with one question: what is the right thing? There was no debate among early philosophers about core values, but there has been one long conversation, stretching over two thousand years, about how to live one's life.

Frankl, an Austrian neurologist and psychiatrist and the founder of logotherapy, is only one of many who have looked at this question, "What is the meaning of life?" When life asks us that question, each of us must answer that question for ourselves. You give to your life meaning and purpose. Or if not, your life will likely be an unpleasant one.

I have an answer for you—not *the* answer, just an answer. For whatever reason, each of us has ten to twenty internal core values. I have shown you how to find them in this book. It is not a big jump to realize that if these are inherent within us and closest to our hearts, then living a life consistent with them could lead to fulfillment and peace of mind. Importantly, it has worked for many. It is not theory.

---

73 Holiday, Ryan. "Why You Should Study Philosophy: Applying the Wisdom of the Ancient Thinkers to the Everyday Problems of Modern Life." Medium.com. June 21, 2019. https://forge.medium.com/why-you-should-study-philosophy-47c53fbc3205.

Philosophy can be one more resource in helping you move from your core values to your goals and how to live your life.

STOICISM: PRACTICAL PHILOSOPHY YOU CAN ACTUALLY USE

Over the past few years, this ancient philosophy has become popular again, not in small part because of Ryan Holiday. Here is an excerpt from his discussion on Stoicism:

> Specifically, I am referring to *Stoicism*, which, in my opinion, is the most *practical of all philosophies*.

> A brief synopsis on this particular school of Hellenistic philosophy: Stoicism was founded in Athens by Zeno of Citium in the early 3rd century B.C., but was famously practiced by the likes of *Epictetus*, *Cato*, *Seneca*, and *Marcus Aurelius*. The philosophy asserts that virtue (such as wisdom) is happiness and judgment be based on behavior, rather than words. That we don't control and cannot rely on external events, *only ourselves and our responses*.

> But at the very root of the thinking, there is a very simple, though not easy, way of living. Take obstacles in your life and *turn them into your advantage*, control what you can and accept what you can't.

—Ryan Holiday[74]

(If you want to learn more about Stoicism or Ryan Holiday, go here: https://dailystoic.com/what-is-stoicism-a-definition-3-stoic-exercises-to-get-you-started/.)

YOU HAVE SOME CONTROL OVER YOUR LIFE

Stoics distinguish between things within our power and those not within our power. There is one thing over which we have *great* control: our core values.

Your core values are part of you. You cannot adopt them. (But remember, you don't "choose" core values. They can only be discovered, as they are inherent within you.)

You certainly have control over trying to live a life consistent with your core values. That's not to say that every decision and action made in this manner will be successful. We do not have control over that, but we can say that when we act in congruence with our core values, we are likely to experience fulfillment and peace of mind, as Hyrum Smith and Covey have taught us.

Why, in a book about core values, have I included all these related yet independent concepts: habits, willpower, the

---

74 Holiday, Ryan. "Actionable Philosophy." *Classical Wisdom Weekly*, May 9, 2014. https://classicalwisdom.com/philosophy/actionable-philosophy/.

Pareto Principle, the Wheel of Life, Aristotle's pursuit of happiness, your "why," following your passion, self-knowledge, essentialism, the Matrix, becoming a philosopher, and Stoicism?

Because core values don't live in a vacuum.

I felt that you may get a better feel for the benefit of core values and how they work if I combined them with other popular or important concepts. Plus, there's a nice synergy with these ideas. Better results come from the combination.

Lastly, I believe in the power of combining other strong ideas with core values.

CHAPTER 12

WHAT OTHERS
HAVE SAID ABOUT
CORE VALUES

When I started writing this book, I was stunned to see so little currently written and discussed about core values. Very few bloggers and writers even mention it today. Their focus is on goals-based systems and productivity hacks. So, much of the teaching that exists on this subject (primarily in the form of books, lectures, and seminars) was done thirty years ago, when my interest in this subject began.

Hyrum Smith and his partner Stephen R. Covey traveled the world, speaking to individuals and corporations about this subject. Their company, FranklinCovey, also played a big role.

I would say Hyrum Smith was the father of this movement. He would disagree. Regardless, he focused on it the most in his day and taught me the most. In many ways, my book is simply a modernization of his teaching.

While writing this book over the past year, I found as many accomplished men and women as I could who talked about the importance of core values (or in some cases, did not use the phrase "core values" but referred to them with other language). I included their words in this chapter. I also chose a few quotes from others simply because I like them.

These quotes go back further than two thousand years. I included what are considered some of the greatest thinkers who ever lived: Seneca, Marcus Aurelius, Leonardo da Vinci, Descartes, Viktor Frankl, and Einstein. Yet, my favorites are those by Hyrum Smith.

ON WILLINGNESS TO CHANGE

Progress is impossible without change, and those who cannot change their minds change nothing.[75]

—GEORGE BERNARD SHAW

Elastic thinking is what you need when the circumstances

---

75 Shaw, Bernard. *Everybody's Political What's What.* New York: Dodd, Mead & Co., 1944.

change and you are dealing with something new. It's not about
following rules.[76]

—LEONARD MLODINOW, AUTHOR OF *ELASTIC*

"Someday" is a disease that will take your dreams to the grave
with you.[77]

—TIM FERRISS, AUTHOR AND PODCAST HOST

You pile up enough tomorrows, and you'll find you've collected
a lot of empty yesterdays.[78]

—MEREDITH WILLSON AND FRANKLIN
LACEY, FROM *THE MUSIC MAN*

Open your arms to change, but don't let go of your values.[79]

—H. JACKSON BROWN, JR.

ON THE SECOND HALF OF LIFE

The psychology of the first half of life is driven by the fantasy
of acquisition…acquiring a standing in the world, whether it
be through property, relationship, or social function. But then
the second half of life asks of us, and ultimately demands, relin-
quishment—relinquishment of identification with property,

76   Shah, Dhruti. "How to become an 'elastic thinker' and problem solver" *BBC Worklife*, May 15, 2018. https://www.bbc.com/worklife/article/20180515.

77   Ferriss, Tim. *The 4-Hour Work Week: Escape 9–5, Live Anywhere, and Join the New Rich.* New York: Crown Publishers, 2007.

78   Willson, Meredith and Franklin Lacey. *The Music Man.* New York: G.P. Putnam's Sons, 1958.

79   Brown, H. Jackson Jr. *Life's Little Instruction Book.* Nashville: Thomas Nelson, 1997.

*roles, status, provisional identities—and the embrace of other,
inwardly confirmed values.*[80]

—DR. JAMES HOLL, *FINDING MEANING
IN THE SECOND HALF OF LIFE*

*The first half of my life I went to school, the second half of my
life I got an education.*

—UNKNOWN

ON READING

*That the perusal of all excellent books is, as it were, to interview
with the noblest men of past ages, who have written them, and
even a studied interview, in which are discovered to us only
their choicest thoughts.*[81]

—RENÉ DESCARTES, *DISCOURSE ON METHOD*

*Contact with writers of genius procures us the immediate
advantage of lifting us to a higher plane; by their superior-
ity alone they confer a benefit on us even before teaching us
anything...They accustom us to the air of the mountaintops.*[82]

—A. G. SERTILLANGES, O.P., *THE INTELLECTUAL LIFE*

80 Hollis, James. *Finding Meaning in the Second Half of Life.* Gotham Books, 2005.

81 Descartes, René. *Discourse on Method.* Translated by John Veitch. Chicago: The Open
Court Publishing Company, 1913.

82 Sertillanges, A.G. *The Intellectual Life: Its Spirit, Conditions, Methods.* Translated by Mary
Ryan. Washington, DC: The Catholic University of America Press, 1987.

As Aristotle noted, "If having some understanding and wisdom is of some advantage to a man, then reading the great books can improve the mind and so help a man in the pursuit of happiness and in the performance of his duties."

The fact that a book is famous is enough to scare off some people who, if they had the courage to open the pages, would find there delight and profit. We make the mistake of fearing that the immortal things of art must be approached through special studies and disciplines, and we comfort ourselves on the principle of sour grapes, by deciding that even if we were prepared to read the classics, we should find them dull. But one explanation of any long fame is that it is deserved, and the men who wrote these books would have been horrified if they had known that you and I might think of them only as matter for school and college courses. They wrote to be read by the general public, and they assumed in their readers an experience of life and an interest in human nature, nothing more.[83]

—JOHN ERSKINE, AUTHOR OF *THE DELIGHT OF GREAT BOOKS*, EDUCATOR, AUTHOR, PIANIST, AND COMPOSER

Our minds, unlike our bodies, are able to grow and develop until death overtakes us. The only condition of its continual growth is that it be continually nourished and exercised. How

---

83   Erskine, John. *The Delight of Great Books*. Indianapolis: Bobbs-Merrill Company, 1928.

nourished? By reading the great books year after year. How exercised? By discussing them.[84]

—MORTIMER ADLER, PHILOSOPHER, EDUCATOR, AND AUTHOR

Think of books as condensed time. Distilled and compressed in the pages of books are years, decades, and even centuries of knowledge and wisdom. If you read a good book, you are concentrating the time you have...A book is always happy to receive a visitor.[85]

—LUCIUS ANNAEUS SENECA, ROMAN STOIC
PHILOSOPHER, STATESMAN, AND DRAMATIST

ON GOALS

For all their bitching about what's holding them back, most people have a lot of trouble coming up with the defined dreams they're being held from.[86]

—TIM FERRISS, AUTHOR AND PODCAST HOST

As I said, to put our faith in tangible goals would seem to be, at best, unwise. So we do not strive to be firemen, we do not strive to be bankers, nor policemen, nor doctors. We strive to

---

84 Adler, Mortimer J. "The Great Books, the Great Ideas, and a Lifetime of Learning." Harvard's Lowell Lecture, April 11, 1990. http://www.radicalacademy.org/adlerlowelllec.html.

85 Gambardella, Steven. "Seneca: Slowing Down Time." *Medium.com*, March 23, 2019. https://medium.com/lessons-from-history/seneca-slowing-down-time.

86 Ferriss, Tim. *The 4-Hour Work Week: Escape 9–5, Live Anywhere, and Join the New Rich.* New York: Crown Publishers, 2007.

be ourselves...In short, he has not dedicated his life to reaching
a pre-defined goal, but he has rather chosen a way of life he
knows he will enjoy.[87]

—HUNTER S. THOMPSON, AUTHOR

Man's ideal state is realized when he has fulfilled the purpose
for which he was born. And what is it that reason demands
of him? Something very easy—that he live in accordance with
his own nature.[88]

—LUCIUS ANNAEUS SENECA

If you always put limits on everything you do, physical or any-
thing else, it will spread into your work and into your life. There
are no limits. There are plateaus, but you must not stay there,
you must go beyond them. If it kills you, it kills you. A man
must constantly exceed his level.[89]

—BRUCE LEE

Why are successful men able to do things they don't like to do
while failures are not? Because successful men have a purpose
strong enough to make them form the habit of doing things

---

87 Thompson, Hunter S. "Transcript of a Letter to Hume Logan, April 22, 1958." In *Letters of Note: An Eclectic Collection of Correspondence Deserving of a Wider Audience,* Compiled by Shaun Usher, 64–68. San Francisco: Chronicle Books, 2013.

88 Seneca, Lucius Annaeus. *Letters from a Stoic: Penguin Classics Edition.* Translated by Robin Campbell and edited by Betty Radice. London: Penguin Books, 1969.

89 Lee, Bruce. *The Art of Expressing the Human Body,* compiled and edited by John Little. Tokyo: Tuttle Publishing, 1998.

they don't like to do in order to accomplish the purpose they want to accomplish.[90]

—ALBERT E. N. GRAY, *THE COMMON DENOMINATOR OF SUCCESS*

Note from the author: Allow me (Roy) to summarize Gray's book: Everyone wants to achieve their goals. However, winners focus on the **prize,** and failures focus on the **price**!

ON SAYING "NO"

It is not daily increase but daily decrease. Hack away at the unessential.

—BRUCE LEE

One note on the definition of personal productivity: By relevant output, I mean working on the right things. You can be highly productive and have a lot of output, but the results you achieve might be useless. When you focus on relevant output, you get the right things done. Things that improve your career, business, organization.[91]

—DARIUS FOROUX, AUTHOR (FOR MORE, I SUGGEST VISITING DARIUSFOROUX.COM, WHERE HE SHARES IDEAS FOR LIVING A PRODUCTIVE LIFE)

---

90 Gray, Albert E. N. *The Common Denominator of Success*. Tremendous Life Books, 2008.

91 Foroux, Darius. "What Is Productivity? A Definition & Proven Ways To Improve It." DariusForoux.com. https://dariusforoux.com/what-is-productivity/.

So why do you do what you do? That's the question you need to answer. Stare at it until you can.

Only then can you understand what matters and what doesn't. Only then can you say no—can you opt out of stupid races that don't matter or exist...Only then you can develop the quiet confidence that Seneca called euthymia—"the belief that you're on the right path and not led astray by the many tracks which cross yours of people who are hopelessly lost."[92]

—RYAN HOLIDAY

The goal is not to simply eliminate the bad, which does nothing more than leave you with a vacuum, but to pursue and experience the best in the world.[93]

—TIM FERRISS, AUTHOR AND PODCAST HOST

ON VALUES

Man is pushed by drives. But he is pulled by values.[94]

—VIKTOR FRANKL, *THE WILL TO MEANING*

92 Holiday, Ryan. "Why Do You Do What You Do? Because You Better Know." ThoughtCatalog.com, February 22, 2020. https://thoughtcatalog.com/ryan-holiday/2014/10/why-do-you-do-what-you-do-because-you-better-know/.

93 Ferriss, Tim. *The 4-Hour Work Week: Escape 9–5, Live Anywhere, and Join the New Rich.* New York: Crown Publishers, 2007.

94 Frankl, Viktor. *The Will to Meaning: Foundations and Applications of Logotherapy.* New York: Penguin, 1988.

Why discover your core values? Because the first step in deploying your authentic self is this: you have to know who you are.[95]

—DAWN BARCLAY

Lasting change is a series of compromises. And compromise is alright, as long your values don't change.[96]

—JANE GOODALL

Try not to become a man of success but rather try to become a man of value.[97]

—EINSTEIN

Vocation does not mean a goal that I pursue. It means a calling that I hear. Before I can tell my life what I want to do with it, I must listen to my life telling me who I am. I must listen for the truths and values at the heart of my own identity, not the standards by which I must live—but the standards by which I cannot help but live if I am living my own life.[98]

—PARKER J. PALMER, FOUNDER OF THE CENTER FOR
COURAGE AND RENEWAL, FROM HIS BOOK *LET YOUR
LIFE SPEAK: LISTENING FOR THE VOICE OF VOCATION*

---

95 Barclay, Dawn. "Core Values." *Living Moxie.* Accessed August 13, 2020. https://dawnbarclay.com/core-values/.

96 Goodall, Jane. "Subject: Jane Goodall, primatologist and conservationist." *Summit Says: Instant Interviews.* World Summit on Sustainable Development, Johannesburg 2002, August 26, 2002. http://www.dailysummit.net/says/interview260802.htm.

97 Miller, William. "Death of a Genius: His fourth dimension, time, overtakes Einstein." *Time,* May 2, 1955.

98 Palmer, Parker J. *Let Your Life Speak: Listening for the Voice of Vocation.* San Francisco: Jossey-Bass, 2000.

When your behavior conflicts with your values, the result is a mental conflict…Your goals will become a reality faster and with less stress if they align with your values.[99]

—TONY JEARY, AUTHOR, *SUCCESS* MAGAZINE, OCTOBER 2016

Maturity also means that you have set your values, that you know what you really want out of life…Not to arrive at a clear understanding of one's own values is a tragic waste…

The standards by which you live must be your own standards, your own values, your own convictions in regard to what is right and wrong, what is true and false, what is important and what is trivial. When you adopt the standards and values of someone else or a community or a pressure group, you surrender your own integrity. You become, to the extent of your surrender, less of a human being.[100]

—ELEANOR ROOSEVELT, AS QUOTED IN *YOU LEARN BY LIVING*

When we choose Should, we're choosing to live our life for someone or something other than ourselves. The journey to Should can be smooth, the rewards can seem clear, and the options are often plentiful.

Must is different. Must is who we are, what we believe, and

---

99 Jeary, Tony. "Do Your Actions Reflect Your Values?" *Success Magazine*, September 19, 2016. https://www.success.com/do-your-actions-reflect-your-values/.

100 Roosevelt, Eleanor. *You Learn by Living: Eleven Keys for a More Fulfilling Life.* Louisville: Westminster John Knox Press, 1960.

what we do when we are alone with our truest, most authentic self. It's that which calls to us most deeply. It's our convictions, our passions, our deepest held urges and desires—unavoidable, undeniable, and inexplicable. Unlike Should, Must doesn't accept compromises.[101]

—ELLE LUNA, *THE CROSSROADS OF SHOULD AND MUST*

Estimate the value of men by the utility of those employments on which they bestow their attention.[102]

—MARCUS AURELIUS

A man who examines the saddle and bridle and not the animal itself when he is out to buy a horse is a fool.[103]

—LUCIUS ANNAEUS SENECA

When your values are clear to you, making decisions becomes easier.[104]

—ROY E. DISNEY, FORMER EXECUTIVE
OF THE WALT DISNEY COMPANY

---

101 Luna, Elle. *The Crossroads of Should and Must: Find and Follow Your Passion.* New York: Workman Publishing, 2015.

102 Antoninus, Marcus Aurelius. *The Meditations of the Emperor Marcus Aurelius Antoninus.* Translated by R. Graves. London: W. Baynes, 1811.

103 Seneca, Lucius Annaeus. *Letters from a Stoic: Penguin Classics Edition.* Translated by Robin Campbell and edited by Betty Radice. London: Penguin Books, 1969.

104 Colan, Lee. "A Lesson from Roy A. Disney on Making Values-based Decisions." *Inc.*, July 24, 2019. https://www.inc.com/lee-colan/a-lesson-from-roy-a-disney-on-making-values-based-decisions.html.

When your days are filled with only those core essentials that mean the world to you—and you're succeeding in those few areas—you absolutely will dominate in all areas of your life. Because the only things in your life are the things you highly value, you're intrinsically motivated by what you're doing.[105]

—BENJAMIN HARDY, AUTHOR

Then, with such security as a person and a grounded sense of competence and self-worth, we can try to pursue our most unique purpose, hone our authenticity and core values, and then, with that strong foundation and knowledge of who we are and what makes our own unique life worth living, we can authentically transcend our selves, contributing our full humanness to increase the human condition.[106]

—SCOTT BARRY KAUFMAN, *SCIENTIFIC AMERICAN*

ON FULFILLMENT, HAPPINESS, AND INNER PEACE

Happiness is that state of consciousness which proceeds from the achievement of one's values…But neither life nor happiness can be achieved by the pursuit of irrational whims.[107]

—AYN RAND

---

105 Hardy, Benjamin. "Why Most People Will Never Be Successful." *Inc.*, October 10, 2016. https://www.inc.com/benjamin-p-hardy/why-most-people-will-never-be-successful.html.

106 Kaufman, Scott Barry. "There Is No One Way to Live a Good Life: Humanistic Psychology Is an Uplifting, Compassionate View of Humanity." *Beautiful Minds* (blog). *Scientific American*, September 21, 2017. https://blogs.scientificamerican.com/beautiful-minds/there-is-no-one-way-to-live-a-good-life/

107 Rand, Ayn. *For the New Intellectual: The Philosophy of Ayn Rand*. New York: Signet, 1968.

As a well-spent day brings happy sleep, so life well used brings happy death.[108]

—LEONARDO DA VINCI

The greatest achievement was at first and for a time a dream. The oak sleeps in the acorn; the bird waits in the egg; and in the highest vision of the soul a waking angel stirs. Dreams are the seedlings of realities...

Tempest-tossed souls, wherever you may be, under whatever conditions you may live, know this—in the ocean of life the isles of Blessedness are smiling, and the sunny shore of your ideal awaits your coming. Keep your hands firmly upon the helm of thought. In the bark of your soul reclines the commanding Master; He does but sleep; wake Him. Self-control is strength. Right thought is mastery. Calmness is power. Say unto your heart, "Peace. Be still."[109]

—JAMES ALLEN, PHILOSOPHER AND WRITER

QUOTES FROM HYRUM SMITH AND STEPHEN R. COVEY

Thirty years ago, Hyrum Smith and Stephen R. Covey wrote and gave seminars on core values all over the world. Hyrum Smith founded Franklin Quest in 1981. Smith cre-

---

108 Da Vinci, Leonardo. *Leonardo Da Vinci's Note-Books.* Translated by Edward McCurdy. London: Duckworth & Co., 1906.

109 Allen, James. *As a Man Thinketh.* Chicago: Sheldon University Press, 1908.

ated the Franklin Planner in 1984. Then in 1997, Franklin Quest merged with the Covey Leadership Center to form FranklinCovey, which is a world leader in helping organizations achieve results that require lasting changes in human behavior.

STEPHEN R. COVEY

It comes from inside-out congruence, from living a life of integrity in which our daily habits reflect our deepest values...

Peace of mind comes from when your life is in harmony with true principles and values and in no other way...

The ability to subordinate an impulse to a value is the essence of the proactive person...Proactive people are driven by values—carefully thought about, selected, and internalized values...

The fourth generation of self-management gives you the opportunity to organize your life to the best of your ability in harmony with your deepest values. But it also gives you the freedom to peacefully subordinate your schedule to higher values. This gives you direction and purpose to the way you spend each day.[110]

---

110 Covey, Stephen R. *The 7 Habits of Highly Effective People.* New York: Free Press, 1989.

Examining your life and facing up to your actual values may be one of the most difficult (though rewarding) experiences of your life...

Everyone has governing values. But those values are unique to the individual...

Once you've identified your unique set of governing values, you've built the foundation of your personal productivity pyramid (or fulfillment pyramid, if you prefer), the larger framework in which your governing values, long-range and intermediate goals, and daily activities can all be focused to help you achieve the thing we all desire in life: inner peace...

Your governing values are the foundation of personal success and fulfillment.[111]

CONCLUSION

Why did I take up an entire chapter with quotes? Quotes can do things that explanatory text cannot. They can inspire and, sometimes, even reach the heart. Isn't it inspiring to read how successful, even brilliant, people have thought about this subject over time?

---

111 Smith, Hyrum W. *The 10 Natural Laws of Successful Time and Life Management: Proven Strategies for Increased Productivity and Inner Peace.* New York: Hachette Book Group, 1994.

CHAPTER 13

———

THE LAST WORD

Now we come to the end of the road. I have explained how and why core values work and how they helped me achieve my life's goals after a rather unimpressive early adult life. (Let's just say that I was a failure.)

You now know how to find your personal core values. I have given you the tools to find out *who you are*. Is this enough?

Is it enough to fulfill Hyrum Smith's promise: if you live life based upon your core values, you will find fulfillment and peace of mind? (Remember that he also told me total freedom, meaning complete financial independence, often follows.)

I would be less than candid if I failed to inform you of this: core values by themselves have not been enough in my life to gain freedom (financial independence). It also takes courage. Twice, I quit companies even though there was great uncertainty. I didn't know whether I would succeed or fail.

I also believe that to give myself the very best chance for freedom, I had to develop these additional talents: people skills, goal-setting habits, discipline, self-examination, self-improvement (mostly through reading), and a good set of morning-stacked habits. There is undoubtedly more, but these are what come to mind.

If I did not develop any one of these talents or skills, I'm not certain if I would be writing this book. Could I have succeeded without people skills or goal-setting ability or courage at key moments? I don't believe so. I *know* that without courage, I certainly would not have succeeded.

Obviously, I don't want to minimize core values. They are critical to success. (Yes: success can be achieved without them, but why would you want to go into battle with one hand tied behind your back?) Unlike the other skills I just mentioned, which can take years of experience and, for some, may not be easily achieved, anyone can discover their inherent core values by using the tools set forth in this book.

If I had not become an aggressive reader, which only happened later in my career, I would have missed books that dealt with this subject and especially the two writers who went into detail about the benefits of using core values in daily life. I would not have studied other achievers and how their success occurred.

I always thought only special people ever gained fulfillment, peace of mind, and financial independence. I learned that is not true. If someone reads enough good books (self-help, literature, histories, biographies by the best writers) and is willing to try new approaches to life, then they can succeed. As long as I focused on social media, most TV, politics, gossip, conspiracies, and entertainment, I didn't go anywhere… When I changed my focus, when I changed what I read, everything changed.

Hyrum Smith made a promise (see below). And now I'm going to make a promise: if you live a life consistent with your core values and apply the learnings from good books, you will have a wonderful opportunity to find fulfillment, peace of mind, and financial independence. That ship is ready to sail. It is waiting for you. Welcome aboard. Bon voyage!

Allow me to leave you with a couple of thoughts that have inspired me. I hope they do the same for you:

Peace of mind comes from when your life is in harmony with true principles and values and in no other way…

—STEPHEN R. COVEY

The secret to achieving inner peace lies in understanding our inner core values—those things in our lives that are most important to us—and then seeing that they are reflected in the daily events of our lives.[112]

This last quote is from Hyrum Smith, the man who changed my life. Hyrum died three weeks after I met with him on his ranch in southern Utah in November 2019. He knew then that he only had weeks to live.

112 Smith, Hyrum W. *The 10 Natural Laws of Successful Time and Life Management: Proven Strategies for Increased Productivity and Inner Peace.* New York: Hachette Book Group, 1994.

ACKNOWLEDGMENTS

I thank the folks who played an important role in my life and, hence, the writing of this book: Ed Murphy, who introduced me to my college fraternity with some wonderful guys, most of whom I still see regularly. The men of Beta Theta Pi (Gamma Mu chapter), who first taught me about fellowship, friendship and teamwork. Tom Shoop, who twice made a huge difference in my career. David Humphrey for my spiritual life. And my parents and sister, Lynell, who were a wonderfully supportive and loving family. The book flowed from what I learned and gained from each of these fine people.

My thanks and appreciation to Scribe Media and the professional folks who made my first and only book happen. They provided the direction and guidance as well as editing essential to its creation:

Paul Fair

Zoe Ratches

Meghan McCracken

Libby Allen

Shannon Lee

Carolyn Purnell

Kevin Quach

Zach Obront

Ellie Cole

Hal Clifford

Rachael Brandenburg

Kelley Heider

BIBLIOGRAPHY

Allen, James. *As a Man Thinketh.*

Aristotle. *The Nicomachean Ethics.* Translated by David Ross. Oxford: Oxford University Press, 2009.

Botton, Alain de. *The Consolations of Philosophy.*

Braham, Barbara J. *Finding Your Purpose.*

Campbell, Joseph. *The Hero with a Thousand Faces.*

Carroll, Lewis. *Alice in Wonderland.*

Clear, James. *Atomic Habits.*

Covey, Stephen. *The 7 Habits of Highly Effective People.*

Dalio, Ray. *Principles.*

Duhigg, Charles. *The Power of Habit: Why We Do What We Do in Life and Business.*

Eurich, Dr. Tasha., *Insight: Why We're Not as Self-Aware as We Think, and How Seeing Ourselves Clearly Helps Us Succeed at Work and in Life.*

Ferriss, Tim. *The 4-Hour Chef.*

Frankl, Viktor. *Man's Search for Meaning.*

Greene, Robert. *Mastery.*

Hall, Dr. Edith. *Aristotle's Way: How Ancient Wisdom Can Change Your Life.*

Hardy, Benjamin. *Personality Isn't Permanent.*

Holiday, Ryan. *The Obstacle Is the Way, Stillness Is the Key.*

Montaigne, Michel de. *Complete Essays.*

Sinek, Simon, David Mead, and Peter Docker. *Find Your Why: A Practical Guide for Discovering Purpose for You and Your Team.*

Smith, Hyrum. *What Matters Most.*

ABOUT THE
AUTHOR

Roy Cook's educational background is in mathematics and engineering physics, but he spent his early career as a marketing manager for Procter & Gamble in Cincinnati. He later became an entrepreneur and ran a national marketing firm that dealt with top fifty blue-chip companies.

Roy's professional life has undergone many evolutions, but he has retained a long-standing interest in how individuals can best achieve fulfillment and peace of mind. The principles that he's developed helped him retire just eleven years after starting his own company. Now, Roy lives in a small town in Northern California with his wife and three cats.